ALSO BY A. G. MOGAN

- Daughter of Paris: *The Diary of Marie Duplessis, France's Most Celebrated Courtesan*
- The S-Bahn Murderer: The Hunt for, and Confession of Paul Ogorzow, Nazi Germany's Most Notorious Serial Killer
- The Secret Journals Of Adolf Hitler: *The Anointed (Volume 1)*
- The Secret Journals Of Adolf Hitler: *The Struggle (Volume 2)*
- Love on Triple W: *A Heartbreaking True Story About Love, Betrayal, and Survival*
- Humorous History: *An Illustrated Collection Of Wit & Irony From The Past*
- Tragic History: *A Collection of Some of the Most Catastrophic Events in Human History*

STALIN'S SNIPER

THE WAR DIARY OF ROZA SHANINA

A. G. MOGAN

WITH ANNOTATIONS BY THOSE WHO KNEW HER

Stalin's Sniper: *The War Diary of Roza Shanina* **/ A. G. Mogan**

For future releases and promotions, or to connect on social media, please visit the author's website at:

www.AGMogan.com

CONTENTS

ACKNOWLEDGMENTS

My first and greatest debt is to the **Arkhangelsk Regional Museum of Local Lore** and to **N.V. Ipatova**, **A.A. Istomin** and **V.P. Mamonov**, the editors and publishers of *The brave girl from Ustya,* the book in which the fullest version of Roza's diary was published in Russian, for giving me permission to translate and use not only Roza Shanina's actual front diary but also the information about her background and the history of the Shanin family.

I'd also like to thank **Andrew Vdovin** for his fastidious work in translating Roza's diary from Russian, for understanding what I really wanted, for his admirable regard to the often difficult, colloquial language of the diary, and for his scrupulous determination to get it right.

Finally, thanks to **William Pope**, who filled in many gaps and allowed me to use his translations of

Roza's death notification and the letters to war correspondent Pyotr Molchanov as well as his information about the fate of Roza's fellow snipers Alexandra Ekimova, Kaleria Petrova, and Dusya Kekesheva.

To those who died so we could be free

FOREWORD

Translated for the first time into the English language by a professional translator, the war diary of Roza Shanina is a unique piece of history. On the one hand, this is because diaries were strictly prohibited in the Soviet military in an effort to preserve secrecy, so there aren't many of them around. Roza was not known for her amenability, but she left behind a fascinating account of her life—though brief as it was—in the trenches of World War II.

On the other hand, not only can we glimpse into the past to a time when war and conflict shaped personalities and turned ordinary men and women into warriors and sometimes heroes, but also experience the war through the eyes of a young—sometimes impressionable, sometimes sensitive, sometimes ruthless—girl. And this makes her diary even more unique.

At times, we see the modest girl unfazed by her popularity:

"Yes, my portrait was in the 'Humor' magazine on November 7. But I am too overrated. I do only what is required of every Soviet soldier, that's all. I am famous everywhere, it's too much."

At other times, we meet a spiritual woman who, besides fighting, took great pleasure in reading, and was able to retain and jot down in her diary passages that inspired her.

"While I was in the recovery center, I read 'Sister Carrie' and 'Bagration.' Good books. 'Oh Carrie, Carrie! Oh blind strivings of the human heart! Onward, onward, it saith, and where beauty leads, there it follows.'"

"Recently, poet Ilya Ehrenburg wrote about me in the army newspaper [...]. I thank her fifty-seven times over. She has saved the lives of thousands of Soviet people. And I thought to myself: 'Is this really glory? Glory is either getting your own skull split in the name of the Motherland, or crushing the skull of someone else —that's what glory is!' (Bagration said), while this is just hogwash for the rear. What I've actually done? No more than I have to as a Soviet man, having stood up to defend the Motherland."

Then, we discover the sensitive, romantic Roza - who despite the brutality and ruthlessness of the surroundings in which she found herself, still possessed a woman's heart, with the woman's needs for attention and affection:

"My heart yearns for a caress."

"My heart is heavy, I'm 20 years old and don't have a close friend, why? There are plenty of guys around, but my heart does not trust any one of them."

"In 8 m[onth]s, four guys kissed me, and not without reason, because I was well familiar with them. There was a period when I went out with two at the same time. This is not good, but it had happened with me as a civilian, too, and it's acceptable for me, because in the depth of her heart every woman is a slut, as a well-known person once said."

But with all spirituality, sensitivity, modesty and romanticism stripped out, we discover a brave—sometimes foolishly so—woman, a courageous spirit who yearned not for caresses and kisses and friends but for action, fighting, and the imminent danger she chased running to the battlefield front lines:

"You know, throughout my life at the front there was not a moment when I didn't long for a fight; I want a fierce fight, want to go with the soldiers. I wish I was born a boy – then no one would have paid any attention to me, no one would have felt sorry for me, and I would have fought with all my heart."

"I'd give anything to go and fight with the soldiers now. Oh lord, why do I have this mysterious nature? I just can't understand, but I really crave, crave a fight, a fierce fight. I will give everything, even my life, only to satisfy this urge. It torments me, I can't sleep."

"But some unknown force is pulling me to the front line. Oh, passion, passion! Oh, blind strivings of the human heart! Onward, onward, it saith, and where *beauty leads, there it follows. I obey my heart. I like adventures, explosions, and it is particularly interesting to repel counterattacks. Whatever happens, I'll charge onward – it's my last irrevocable charge!"*

Roza's diary was handed to Pyotr Molchanov, a war correspondent, by the staff of the 205th medical battalion's hospital, wherein Roza died. She and Molchanov had been friends, keeping frequent correspondence with each other during the war. Molchanov kept Roza's diary—which consisted of three thick notebooks—in his Kiev apartment for twenty years, before allowing a heavily edited version to be published by the journal "Yunost" in 1965.

Later, Roza Shanina's diary was deposited in the Arkhangelsk Regional Museum of Local Lore. On April 29, 2010, the diary was passed on to the Ustya Museum of Local Lore, which obtained the agreement of Roza Shanina's closest relative—her brother Marat Yegorovich Shanin—who approved the publication.

The diary you are about to read in this book is the newest version—in as full a form as possible, more accurate and more complete. It has never been published in full. According to Marat Shanin, Roza's brother, "it would be right to include everything that Roza wrote in the diary, unless there are fragments that look immoral or offensive."

I was tempted to make the entire book a historical novel, but after much consideration, I decided to leave the text of the diary untouched. I did not find it in my heart to take away from it, as fictionalization often does, so I kept the text of the actual diary in italics while keeping fictionalization to the minimum; it is meant to acquaint readers with Roza's background, life before the war, family, friends and acquaintances as well as what those people thought or said about her—thoughts which are expressed in this book as annotations.

On a final note, I truly hope you enjoy reading about the front line life of this beautiful Soviet sniper during World War II. She was credited with fifty-nine confirmed kills, all committed in the name of the Soviet Union—her Motherland.

THE WAR DIARY OF ROZA SHANINA

With Annotations

by Those Who Knew Her

"I don't want to die... I've seen so little and done so little..."

— Roza Shanina, a day before she died

EPIGRAPHS & POEMS

Roza Shanina's original diary begins with the following epigraphs and poems, so it is best to retain the order in which her entries have been made.

> *"Love stands strong, it gives beauty*
> *where there is none, and forges*
> *chains which no spell can break ..."*
> *("The Heart of a Princess")*

> *"Oh, passion, passion! Oh, blind*
> *strivings of the human heart!*
> *Onward, onward, it saith, and where*
> *beauty leads, there it follows."*
> *("Sister Carrie" by Theodore*
> *Dreiser)*

> *"What is glory? It is either getting your*

own skull split in the name of the
Motherland, or crushing the skull of
someone else ..." (Bagration)

"You would bind my will with your
laws? The law makes a crawling
snail of those who would take off in
an eagle's flight." ("The Story of my
Life" – Rebels' words, a quotation
from The Robbers, a tragedy by
Friedrich Schiller.)

My love

You write to me with resentment that I have forgotten
you.
But you must understand, I am at war, my love.
There are so very many people waiting for my letters:
In Omsk and in Tomsk, my love.
And there is also my lawful wife waiting for me,
I am bound to forget you, my love.
You write to me you already have a daughter that looks
like me,
So let her grow, that's fine with me, my love.
And if someone asks you where the baby's father is,
Say that he died at the front, my love.
Forgive me for that joke, it's the war that's to blame,
And don't wait for me anymore, my love.
Although I'm very proud of you, my family is waiting
for me.

I'm not coming back to you, my love.

* * *

It's midnight outside, the candle is burning down,
Stars can be seen high in the sky.
You are writing me a letter, my darling,
To be sent to an address flaming in the war.
How long you've been writing, my darling!
When you finish, you'll start over again.
But I'm sure that your big love
Will break through to the front line.
We left home long ago, and the light of our rooms
Cannot be seen behind the smoke of war.
But he who is loved and remembered
Feels like home even in the smoke of war.
Your tender letters make me feel warmer at the front:
As I read every line, I can see
My love and I can hear my homeland,
Like a voice behind a thin wall.
We will soon be back, I know and believe,
And the time will come
When sadness and separation will be left behind
the door
And only joy will enter the house.
And one evening, you and me together,
Shoulder to shoulder,
Will sit down and read the letters again
Like annals of war, like a chronicle of our feelings.

To my beloved

I greet you, my beloved, as before,
I do not want to hurt you,
I am still as kind and tender,
Only I look more severe.
Never mind that my character has become stronger
And my way of speaking has become somewhat coarse.
War has new laws to teach us,
And I've gotten used to its laws.
Here in battle we do not fear cold
Or the pounding of heavy fire;
And I'm still the same as before,
It is easy to recognize me among all the others.
Under the melody of bullets and shells whistling,
I'm going to fight again today,
In my once-new overcoat
That I wore when we stood there together, remember?
Hating the enemy with all my heart,
I will go forward like a hero,
So that you and me could happily
Live a free life again.
In the meantime, my love, believe me,
I have to go, I hear the rumble in the distance.
I'm going there to challenge death
In the vast land of fire.
And when I come back from this battle,
Wait for me, do not grieve without reason.
I'll reward you with my greetings
And a fiery hot kiss

* * *

If your soul is filled with sadness,
If a fierce battle breaks out,
I want you to see in a dream and remember
All that we had and did together.
Don't let it get to your head
That we can never meet again,
Remember all the jolly moments we had
And take them on the road with you.
And, as you go into the land of war,
The blood-drenched land,
Know that my love will follow you
Through the misty fields ....

4 OCTOBER 1944

Yesterday, a trenches comrade asked me what my first memory was. We were lying face-up in a ditch and had been silently watching the blue firmament for some time. I laughed and told him that thinking of home, of the families we left behind, and rummaging through memories would do us, soldiers, no good. It would soften us, render us weak. It wasn't the time to be weak, I told him.

He insisted and pressed me to tell him what he had asked with the endearing sweetness of a child who begs for a goodnight story. I again laughed, and gave him the same answer. Then, I told him I was cold and retired to the barracks.

But the damage had already been done. The longing my comrade's question brought about stuck to my heart so firmly that thoughts about my first memory were the only thoughts going around in my mind. Like those leeches ever climbing our uniforms, my longing and thoughts had to be removed, burned. It is a soldier's only shot. His only metaphorical shot. Stay focused or be dead.

Resolving to remain focused and thus alive, I made a pact with myself. I would write down my memories, my thoughts, my feelings for no more than an hour each night, then proceed to forget about them and myself until the next evening. Except for that hour, I would belong to my country alone.

To my sniper rifle.

5 OCTOBER 1944

My first memory is as political as these trenches. As nationalistic as my profession. And as I now look back, it appears like a memory that seemed to have set the course of my life. Like a prophecy.

My father was a very respected man in our village. A very resourceful man. And though he was illiterate—he did not attend a single day of school—I always felt, ever since I can remember, that if I had a question or needed help in learning something new, he was the person to go to. I was about four years old when the sudden curiosity regarding my name came over me. So, one day, I asked my mother why she named me Roza. Somewhat disappointed with her answer, I approached my father, who was chopping fresh logs in the backyard of our house. I pulled him by his pants to stop him from what he was doing and made him look at me. He appeared irritated by my intrusion, but I looked up at him with stubborn determination.

"Father, why am I Roza?" I asked. For a moment he looked confused by my inarticulate question, but then burst into laughter, and placing the axe against the pile of logs he lifted me in his arms and walked to sit on the steps at the rear of the house.

"First of all," he began, "you must know that your name carries much weight. I chose it, as it were, against your mother's wishes."

"Yes, mommy told me. But then she said she began loving it for it means 'rose'. She said that after five boys —my older brothers—I came into her life with the beauty and delicacy of a flower."

My father laughed and ruffled his hair with stiff fingers. "Yes, she kept telling herself that and in time she came to warm to it, but it was not so in the beginning."

"Why?"

"Because she knew I chose it to honor the great communist revolutionary, Roza Luxemburg. She said it was a bad omen."

"Why?"

"Because she was killed too young. Executed by the German Freikorps."

"Why?"

But my father no longer answered my question. He already had been transported by his aggressive nature into one of his dark moods. Moods that sometimes lasted for hours, and in which he would harangue, castigate, and curse some invisible political opponents known only to him. Moods I dreaded and feared.

And this is my first memory. The second was more like a feeling. A feeling telling me I should like to live up to my weighty name.

6 OCTOBER 1944

I met Gudkov, w[ho] had been with Sergey in the Bryansk forest in Belorussia. He asked me to remind Sergey about the town of Kosino where he had happened to be drinking when the bombing began. Now I'm at the newspaper office. It's kind of odd to see people (Olga) thinking about the front line in such a foolish manner, even though they are only 25 kilometers away from the front. Oh, it's hard to live in such a situation! (At the Shushupa river.)

What is also hard, I notice, is keeping my word about the vow I made. It is as if this little notebook screams to come out of my uniform pocket with every chance it gets. So, waiting patiently at the newspaper office, here I take it out again. It's getting addictive.

My thoughts fly now to Sergey, my oldest brother, who has fought the Nazis in the same war as me. I almost put on the weeps on hearing Gudkov talk about him, for it is many months now since I haven't seen him. And I grieve for his troubles. So much grief.

Tall and handsome, with light blond hair and sky-blue eyes, Sergey was born to my family on Christmas Day. Family pictures show him a chubby bundle with a thousand ringlets upon his head. An angelic sweetness like that of baby Jesus with whom he shares his birth day.

He was only twenty-one when he became a member of the Communist Party. All of us children were communists in mind and spirit from a very early age. Father wanted this, and drilled his doctrine into our little heads with a fervor and fanaticism only he possessed. We were never put to sleep with sweet fairy tale stories like were other children, but with stories experienced by Father during the First World War, which he joined three years after Sergey was born.

"Here!" Father would boast, slapping his right leg which wouldn't bend at the knee and was six centimetres shorter than the other. His lame leg was all he took from the war. And his ensuing nickname: Yegor the Lame. "I wasn't yet a veteran when this knee was shattered by a bullet. I would have bled to death if it wasn't for Martynov who dragged me away from the front line after nightfall."

We listened in awe as he continued. "I was taken to the hospital in Odessa, where a doctor wanted to amputate my leg as soon as I arrived. I fought against such a terrible decision, and as luck would have it, they managed to save it. Then they sent me to the hospital in

Moscow where I spent most of 1917. And it was there where I became, for the first time in my life, a devout communist. When a grand duke with his retinue visited the hospital to award us medals and crosses, I pulled my blanket over my face. When the retinue walked away from my bed, I heard one of the noblemen say, 'He's a Bolshevik!' I remember asking myself what a Bolshevik was. I didn't know a thing about Bolsheviks. But then all that changed with the arrival of soldiers, workers and sailors who were injured in the street fights. And it was they who taught me everything about communism and Bolsheviks. That Moscow hospital was my communist university."

Thinking back now, I realize Father's bedtime stories were *my* communist university. And thus I decided, at an age where little girls still play with dolls, that I was to be a fighter. That when I grew up, I would very much love to fight for my beliefs. For a country I loved like nothing else. Just like Roza, the heroine whose name I carried.

8 OCTOBER 1944

I flew with Gudkov on a plane for the first time in my life. Now we are in the 215th Rifle Division with Kozyryan. I miss the 338th [Rifle Division]. *It seems people there are not the same at all. I can't do bad work, or else my conscience would torture me, but it's hard because of all this newspaper rigmarole, the girls are jealous and spreading rumors about me. I'm morally killed.*

Yes. Morally killed. Or injured. I find it so much harder to make friends here with sniper girls. Their jealousy and envy are pitiful. Girls shall be girls, no matter how manly the rifles they carry. I should have gotten used with their mediocrity by now, as girls always seemed to have envied me. I remember my school years... my classmates gossiping about my boyish manners and conduct. I would just laugh and mind my own business.

But not all girls were stupid. When I started primary school, I had to move twelve kilometres from home to the village of Bereznik, where I would live in the house of Mrs. Borisova. One of my classmates, A. Kozlova, lived there with me. Kozlova and I became good friends. We shared everything together. Our landlady worked on a farm as a pig-tender, and after school we would go help her by carrying water, sawing firewood, and feeding the animals. It was a happy carefree time.

A. Kozlova, Roza's friend:

Roza was tall, always trim, brave. She didn't like being idle. She was straightforward by nature and spoke in an open manner. I remember the following incident: one day a few guys from our class got into the collective farm vegetable garden and did some mischief. It became known at school, but the mischief-makers didn't want to own up. Then Roza went to the director and told him everything.

A. Poloskova, Roza's classmate:

Roza was right. We were envious and jealous of her because she was somehow different from the rest of us. Back then we thought of her as arrogant. But it simply was her confident, head-strong nature and a quiet knowledge of belief in herself and her destiny. She knew what she wanted and was the only one among the girls in the 7th grade who attended shooting classes and had a Young Sharpshooter badge as a person who had reached qualifying standards.

Roza was a strong-willed, spry girl. She tried to make her personality and mannerisms more boyish. She wore modest clothes and liked playing volleyball. I liked her straightforward attitude: she didn't like acting against her conscience, and she demanded the same from her friends. If she saw any injustice, she'd tell you about it right on the spot.

A. Makaryin, Roza's teacher:

Roza was indeed a character. So much so that she inspired me to write a verse about her:

> Her nature was headstrong from an
> early age,
> On the other hand, she'd never betray a
> friend.
> She could prickle like a thorn bush,
> And she could always shut down a
> bully.
> In games, she had the same temper,
> Running barefoot like a whirlwind.
> When she grew bigger, she decided to
> study in the city
> And walked 200 kilometres to get
> there.

Marat Shanin, Roza's youngest brother:

I remember we were sawing wood with her. I couldn't keep pulling the saw without any respite. Roza warned me once, then again, and then — bang! — hit me on the hat, unable to hold her temper in check any longer! Well, I had to show her I was no wuss. I grabbed a stick and dashed after her as fast as I could. [We made one] circle around our Commune house, then she dove into a passageway behind it. I followed her, but she was stronger and ran away!

Roza Shanina:

At fourteen years old, after finishing the seven-year school in Bereznik, without my father's permission and with hardly any money or belongings, I resolved to leave the village forever. The choice of my destination was the city of Arkhangelsk, situated almost two thousand kilometres away, in the north of European Russia. Lying on both banks of the Northern Dvina River near its exit into the White Sea, it was said to be the gem of Russia, a beauty to behold. But to be able to see it with my very own eyes, I had to first get myself to the nearest railway station. And the nearest railway station was two hundred kilometres away from the village. But I did not fret. I simply tied my boot laces and walked the two hundred kilometres.

I forgot how many days had passed before I arrived in the city. Starved and on the verge of collapse, I rang the bell to Sergey's home. My brother had moved to Arkhangelsk eight years prior, upon his entrance in the Arkhangelsk Forest Engineering Institute. He was now married and had two daughters. It was upon my arrival to his home that day that I met his family.

The door was opened by his young beautiful wife. With a big smile upon her lips, she asked me to come in.

"I am Raisa," she said, closing the door and rushing to hug me. Over her shoulder, I saw her little daughters, looking suspiciously in my direction.

"And these must be my nieces," I said, letting go of their mother and squatting to be at the same level with the girls.

"Yes. Emma and Roza," said the wife. I hugged them both, while Raisa explained how Sergey insisted on naming his youngest daughter after me. Tears came into my eyes and I let them fall unbridled.

A month after my arrival, I was admitted to the Youth Communist League. At fourteen years old, I was the youngest in my family to become a communist. This was the result of my father's many years of instructive stories, as well as a culmination of my own patriotic dreams.

At about the same time, after successfully passing all examinations, I was admitted to the Arkhangelsk Pedagogical College. So I quit my brother's house for the College dormitory.

A.G. Malysheva, Roza's roommate at the Pedagogical College:

Foolhardily brave, Roza was our friend. She could give a hard time to anybody, even to the boys who offended her, whether unintentionally or deliberately. Staying late at her relatives' or friends' from the Ustyansky District, she would return to the dormitory at 2:00 or 3:00 o'clock in the morning. Of course, all the doors were locked at such a late hour. We would tie a few bed sheets together, and she would climb this "rope" to get in through the window.

Roza Shanina:

Soon after I started my studies, the secondary education institutions introduced tuition fees, while reducing scholarship funds. I had no choice but to look for a job. If I wanted to support myself during my studies, I needed to earn some cash. Thus, on September 11, 1941, I was hired as a kindergarten teacher at the Kindergarten 2 of the Pervomaysky School District, where I would work a few hours a day in the evening class.

T.V. Kurochkina, the director of Kindergarten 2:

[Roza was] a tall, slim girl with pleasant sky-blue eyes and a fresh complexion. She had two fair plaits hanging over her shoulders. Later I found out that her blue eyes could shoot lightning bolts too, and then her face would change in a flash. Her clothes were remarkably simple: a plain cotton dress or, much more often, a grey flannelette sports suit.

[At first Roza was] somewhat sluggish, even stiff. I came to the class in the evening, shortly before supper (at 7 p.m.). Roza wasn't in the class, but the children were playing peacefully. When I asked where their teacher was, they pointed to the sleeping room and said, 'There.' I entered the sleeping room. Roza was sitting at the small table. There was a textbook on the table, and Roza, her arms and head on the book, was fast asleep. I called to her quietly, and she jumped up immediately; when she saw me, her eyes were so full of shame and pain that I didn't have the heart to give her a severe rating. <...> [She] had to sacrifice her night's sleep to do her homework. That's what explained her stiffness.

Roza Shanina:

It was soon thereafter that the peaceful happiness in my brother's family was shattered. By now a state security sergeant serving in the NKVD office for the Arkhangelsk Region, Sergey was arrested on charges of unlawful methods of investigation, beating the accused and falsification of interrogation protocols of the accused and witnesses. The Military Tribunal sentenced him to eight years in jail with deprivation of his special rank.

But then, only a few months into his detention,

with the war in full swing, Sergey was released from the Kuybyshev prison. In a letter sent to his wife he said:

> "I do the same job as before March 1, the only difference being that I used to work on the periphery, while now I'm in the central office. The Commissariat has granted me a leave, and now I'm resting in Kuybyshev. I assure you that my bullets aimed at the enemy will be just as hot as my hatred of the Nazis. I will live up to the confidence reposed in me by the government and justify the noble title of warrior of the USSR. I'm going to the front, and I'll most probably stay there for quite a long time. Don't be perplexed if there are no letters from me. Don't worry about me. I will fight against the Nazis and uphold the honor of our patriotic and communist family."

Thus, in April, 1942, Sergey was already behind enemy lines, as chief intelligence officer in a special NKVD detachment called "Forward", a sabotage and reconnaissance group created by the USSR NKGB for carrying out special missions behind enemy lines. My heart swelled with pride—but also with envy, for I now wanted to be behind enemy lines more than ever.

With this burning desire firmly planted in my heart, I began knocking on every public office door I could find, begging the officials to send me to the front. But being only seventeen years old, my applications were always denied. And if that weren't enough, I soon learned that my employer at the kindergarten, Mrs. T.V. Kurochkina, was doing her best to get me exempted from military service.

T.V. Kurochkina:

Roza said that it was out of the question and that I couldn't do anything of the kind. It was then that I noticed for the first time that her eyes could dart lightning bolts.

Roza Shanina:

But I could not change the fact that I was still a minor, so all I could do was give myself over to military training and practicing my skills to the point of exhaustion. It was a way to let my fury out, and it worked. In a matter of weeks, I became so good at shooting that I could hit a pebble thrown up in the air.

Two years passed, time in which I had continued with stubborn determination to knock on official doors. At last, on June 22nd, 1943, two months after I turned nineteen, I was drafted by the Pervomaysky District Recruitment Office in Arkhangelsk and ordered to the Central Women's Sniper Training School of the Young Communist League Central Committee, located in Podolsk, Moscow Region.

I began packing at once. But there was someone I ached to see before my departure to the capital.

9 OCTOBER 1944

I remember the meeting with my mother as if it happened yesterday. On the morning of my departure to Moscow, I had called her and asked her to come to the village of Shangaly, in the Ustyansky region, which was on my way. There was no time to go home. My cousin Olga was living in an old office building in that village, near the recruitment office. And it was there that I met my mother.

It was a bright day, filled with warmth and hopes. My dream was about to come true, and I was in the best of moods. I woke before the sun, jumped into my soldier shirt and kirza boots, and by 6:00 o'clock in the morning I was already entering the village. Yet Mother had to walk the entire thirty-six kilometres from our home, and she reached Shangaly only just before sunset.

I decided to spend the day visiting some of my

friends, and then went to see Raisa and my nieces. They were very happy to see me, but as we hugged Raisa began crying. Alarmed, I asked her for the cause of her torment. She said Sergey was again arrested, only a few days prior, in Moscow. I was stunned and pressed her for more details. But she didn't know much. It was six months later that we all learned my brother had been sentenced to ten years of imprisonment in a labor camp, on charges of failure to follow orders during wartime, authority abuse, exceeding authority and failing to exercise it, and neglect of official duty in particularly aggravating circumstances. As the chief intelligence officer of the "Forward", he avoided performing his duties. After crossing the front line into the German-occupied territory in April 1942, to conceal his inactivity, Sergey would misinform the USSR NKGB, supplying in his reports and radio messages falsified data concerning the personal identities and number of agents and special mission performance as well as inventing intelligence data and taking credit for operations of the local partisan squads that had no communication with Moscow.

I did not want to believe a word of what I was being told. But his guilt was proven by witness statements and other evidence, and my brother himself also made a confession. I was no longer proud, but stunned and saddened. I was, for days, in complete disbelief about what was happening.

. . .

Leaving my sister-in-law to fight with her own disbelief and sadness, I returned to the house of my cousin Olga and sat on the porch. The excitement and nervousness I now felt, knowing I would soon see my mother—as well as eagerness to set aside the worry I felt for my brother—made me think of her, of our past. Rather short in height, she is the most persistent, selfless, friendliest and calmest person I know; the perfect contrast to Father's nature. And this must have kept them together for so long, these very complementary traits they share that made them surpass all misfortunes and raise a family of seven children. They raised us with the serenity of a loving mother balanced by the sternness of an authoritarian father. I closed my eyes and sighed deeply. This action almost made me feel the smell of her freshly baked bread invading my nostrils.

It wasn't, though, until I saw her silhouette rushing toward me from the cornfield and heard the panting of that dear woman who had walked thirty-six kilometres to meet me, that tears gathered in my eyes. I stood up from the porch steps and rushed to embrace her. The panting of the frail woman intensified my tears.

"Mama..." I cried, enveloped suddenly by that maternal warmth I had forgotten. I had forgotten how much I have missed it.

"Roza, my child," she said in a soothing yet breathless voice.

"Come, rest here," I said, and guided her to the porch steps. "Sit here." She sat, and I next to her. We were both silent for a few minutes, I to let Mother catch her breath, her to stare at me with searching eyes.

"You are so beautiful, my child," Mother said, breaking the silence first. "But too thin. Are you taking care of yourself, Roza? Eating properly, sleeping enough?"

"Yes, Mamochka. You mustn't worry for me. I am no longer a child," I replied with a warm gentle smile.

"You shall be my child to my grave. And you are a child. You are nineteen, my dearest daughter. And look at your hair!"

I ruffled my hair with stiff fingers. "What about it?"

"It's too short." She smiled and reached to caress my face. "It makes you look even younger than your age. And boyish. You always insisted in making yourself look boyish."

I smiled at her words. She is the only person in this world who knows me better than myself. "How is Papa?"

She twisted her face into a scowl. "Papa is...Papa. You know how he is. Some people never change, my child, no matter how much we pray for it."

"And Yuliya?" I asked about my only sister, the youngest in our family.

"She'll be twelve next month. I am terrified by how beautiful she's becoming. She's already almost as tall as you. And very bright."

"Is she continuing her studies? I did not teach her to read and write for nothing. She's the brightest of us all. *Give Yuliya an education, Mamochka. Children are a joy.*"

Mother smiled and took me in her arms. "Look at you, my tomboy, speaking of children being a joy... I never thought I would hear those words coming from your sweet mouth."

"Yes, I never thought that either," I said, with a sudden feeling of melancholy grabbing me. "So young and carefree. And look at me..." I took Mother's hands in mine and began crying. "It is almost a certainty I am going to war," I said. "It is what I want, make no mistake. But what if..." I couldn't continue. The tears were choking me.

"Now, now. What if what?" Mother asked in her soothing voice I knew too well.

"Well... what if I never see you again? What if I die, Mama?" My voice was now distorted by the annoying weakness that made itself known to me with such eagerness.

Mother arose from the porch steps and kneeled in front of me. Taking my hands into hers, which were burning, and looking at me with startling assurance she said, "My children don't die. God wouldn't allow it."

I scoffed, and then told her that her faith in God wasn't enough, and that sometimes good people die for no apparent reason, and against all prayers and divine supplications.

"Listen to me well, Roza. I shall tell you a story. When the First World War began, your father went to the front, as you well know. The only people left in our house were his disabled father and his mother who looked after your brother Sergey, who was at that time only three years old. So, even though I was pregnant with Pavel, I had to do all the heavy work alone. So I went into the field, day by day, until the fall came. And on the first day of September, there I was, swinging my sickle, when suddenly, wouldn't you know it, I had to give birth! So I delivered a boy, wrapped him in my kerchief and some rags I had, and put him on the ground near a stack of straw. I glanced at the sun: it was already high in the sky, and there was so much grain to reap yet! I took my sickle again and went back to work, putting up one stack after another. Dusk began to fall, the shadows of the forest trees had grown longer. I straighten myself up and searched for the stack where I had left the baby. What I saw made me shudder. A herd of cattle that was returning from the pastures was moving along right through the field! Good Lord, I thought, they must have trampled my boy! I dashed to the stack and found my dear little one safe and sound right where I had left him. He didn't even cry. My heart swelled with compassion. I took him in my arms and carried him home. So you see, my dear daughter, my children do not die before their time. It is ordained from above."

My tears dried up, and in my mind I thanked God for this woman, for she was the only breathing person who could calm my fears. And even though I knew she was against her daughter going to war, she never said a word. Her confidence, her assuredness in the existence of a protective higher power watching over her children was enough for her. So I resolved it should be enough for me as well.

As darkness enveloped us both, I hugged Mother with all the love I felt in my heart for her, and made my way toward the train station.

Once on the train, I met my cousin Alexander. He was going to the front and wept alone by the window all the way to Moscow. I never understood why. Was he crying for the family and friends he left behind? Or was he scared? I felt a sudden urge to go tell him that the children in the Shanin family do not die before their time. But for some mysterious reason I kept to my spot in the train and let him be.

Once in Moscow, I was immediately enrolled at the Central Women's Sniper Training School as a new cadet. It was not easy learning there, but my progress was *not bad*, and by the end of the month I took my military oath. I now was ready; ready to see my lifelong dream opening up before my very wide-open eyes.

T. V. Kurochkina, Roza's employer at the kindergarten:

I received a letter from Roza when she was at the Sniper School, in which she described how she had celebrated the New Year being on vacation. They had made decorations and trimmed the New Year tree. Roza made her friends sing children's songs and dance in a ring. It was so much fun. She also said that she was offered to be an instructor at the school, but she refused to stay behind and, reduced in rank, went off to the front.

Roza Shanina:

On the eve of my twentieth birthday, April 2nd, 1944, I arrived at the 45th Rifle Corps of the 5th Army of the 3rd Belorussian Front.

10 OCTOBER 1944

The Germans retreated, and we are going forward and to the left. I met Kozyryan, Major General, hero of the Soviet Union. *They say he's kind to girls. He may not be kind, I don't care, I only hope he's not a womanizer. I remember Gorodovikov,* yet another hero of our Motherland. As the Commander of the 184th Rifle Division of the 45th Rifle Corps of the 5th Army, he took part in the Operation Bagration, in which the 206th German Infantry Division near Vitebsk was defeated. He captured around three thousand soldiers and officers together with their commander, and, chasing the enemy, entered the territory of the Lithuanian Soviet Socialist Republic. After successfully cutting across the Neman, it was the first Soviet division that reached the State Border between the USSR and Germany near Naumiestis. *Kozyryan and Gorodovikov just can't be compared. It's so hard ...*

Whatever happens, I'm not going to be the one they expect me to be (a silly girl).

I had a dream about my brother Fedya.

He is still missing. The thought that he might have been killed by the Nazis makes me writhe in pain. It also doubles the hate I feel for those blasted Fritzes[1]. Poor Fedya... he yearned for the front as much as we all did. But the women in our village told our mother, 'Alexeyevna! You have two lads studying in the city already. Let the third one plough. We don't have enough men to be at the plough.' So poor Fedya had to plough. He was so kind, and loved horses so much...

Marat Shanin, Roza's youngest brother:

I saw Fedya working in the plots at Garnaya. In winter, they carried logs along the frozen crust. The road was watered on purpose. You can put more logs in the sledge when the horse pulls it along the tracks. There was a fairly steep slope, and I saw Fedya sitting in the sledge and holding the reins, sliding along pretty fast. I was scared for him.

But, as he grew up, he remembered his first love: education and the front. He went to Arkhangelsk and entered the workers' faculty at the Arkhangelsk Forest Engineering Institute. In summer vacations he would return home and I, being the youngest, would follow him everywhere like a dog. I would watch him swim across the Ustya River from the bank and would tremble in fear. He was so strong and so brave

—a sportsman, the strongest of all the Shanin brothers.

Then, in July 1939, Fedya graduated from the workers' faculty in Arkhangelsk. He came home, knowing that he had to go off to serve in the Red Army. I was at the Young Pioneer camp in Stroyevskoye. He came to Stroyevskoye to see me and say goodbye. I don't remember what we talked about, I only remember Fedya say, 'I'm going into the army!' I didn't think much of it: all young men serve in the army, anyway... We didn't talk long. Fedya leaned over the weak fence, hugged me, his 11-year-old brother, somewhat awkwardly, and kissed my blond head. Just then I saw his eyes full of tears. Fedya felt we would never see each other again.

In November, he was enlisted for active military service, and assigned to the 25th Chapayev division that took part in the liberation campaign of the Red Army in Bessarabia. He was an artillery man in a howitzer battery. But then, Fedya was wounded: first his eyes were damaged, and then, by a shell fragment in his neck. He was evacuated by sea as critically wounded. Fedya was on a ship, wrapped in a blanket; they wanted to throw him overboard, but he was still breathing, so he was delivered to Georgia, where he had already taken treatment, as I remember from earlier childhood days. He wrote us a letter asking us to send him some clothes: coat, pants, shirt, boots and a piece of outerwear – a padded jacket, probably. And Yegor the Lame, our father, told me, 'Maratko! Write to Fedya.

Let the doctors decide where he should go – back to the front or back home.' Fedya went to the front again ...

He wrote personally to me, because he knew I wanted to become an artist (a painter). So he wrote: 'Marat! If you want to be a good painter, you have to take pains. You must strive and study hard. We're going to have a big battle tomorrow.' Both letters came home to the Commune on the same date. But then, there were no more letters. Ever.

Roza Shanina:

My heart is heavy, I'm 20 years old and don't have a close friend, why? There are plenty of guys around, but my heart does not trust any one of them. It's because of the scumbags who conduct such way of life: they just get what they want from a girl and don't give a damn about her anymore.

They say that girls won't be allowed into Germany, but we are already on the border. Where will fate take us? I remember Mishka Ponarin, Senior Sergeant in the 338th Rifle Division... What a good guy. He has been killed ... He loved me, I know, and I loved him too. Senior Sergeant, with 2 academic years, well-behaved, humble, decent, nice guy. I feel very sorry for him. Our superiors didn't allow him to keep company with me. Starting from the major and above, there is a lot of food ("if ..."), but I'm not that low. I take their presents with one hand and pay them back by slapping their face with the other.

In my mind's eye I see Blokhin and Solomatin. I liked them, but I knew it was only temporary. They left and didn't write any letters – that's the proof. After the 338th Rifle Division I was in the Corps. I hardly knew anyone in the 184th Rifle Division, maybe just a little – superficially and in a comradely way.

Yashka Gudkov pays court to me quite well. Oh, how much injustice! Take the girls, for example. Sasha Yekimova, my friend and fellow sniper in the female sniper platoon squad, 184th Rifle Division. *When I have success, she is friendly. When I don't, she is gone. I am now enjoying great prestige, and she is with me. I don't like this. I want friends like those I had before: Agniya in grades 5-7 or Valya Chernyaeva from courses 1-3 in college. I can't find such a friend here, no. She's a real egoist, and this trait of hers is so irreconcilably antagonistic to my own nature. Dusya Kekeshova,* another fellow sniper. *I like her personality most of all, but she won't make friends with me; we used to be friends, but I betrayed her when Sasha Y. offered me her friendship. She swore to be a good friend, even though there had been some dirty tricks between her and Kalya, and I believed there wouldn't be anything like that anymore, but alas! Dusya hates me for betraying her. Kalya Petrova,* the private 1st class, *refuses to be a friend at all. Shares what she knows with each of us, having no secrets from anyone, that's what Sasha taught her to do, and she made her peace [illegible].*

Kalya Petrova:

It saddens me to learn Roza's thoughts about me. I really liked her and was in awe of her resourceful nature while we studied together at the Sniper School. She would show initiative and use tricks to make the hard army life easier. In winter we were to use skis. We had to go down a gully on skis and then up again, all the while carrying the sniper rifles on our shoulders. Under no circumstances could you fall, otherwise you risked ruining the purpose. It was quite a difficult task, taking into account that not all the girls were very good at skiing. Then Roza suggested using a trick. There was a village near the gully. We were to leave our skis in the yard of the first house, then go down the gully with ease, carefully holding our rifles. On our way back from the shooting range we would take our skis again, put them on and enter the school premises triumphantly. However, this trick was soon discovered, and we had to continue with the full training program. But she was smart. Roza was smart that way.

---

1. Nazis.

12 OCTOBER 1944

I'm beginning my journey, like back in July. We headed for Sberki, 20 km to the left of Sloboda and the Shushupa river. We got in a truck without permission. It broke down near the 184th Sniper Division, and we all went to see our acquaintances there. It was almost evening. I and Kaleriya Petrova spent the night with my fellow countryman, the head of the Political Department. We had a general's dinner, and they wanted us to 'pay' for it, but we're not that kind of girls. In the morning, they put us in a Willys jeep. But we didn't know where to go. Then we met an army car and found out everything. The other girls had spent the night on the front line, there was an attack and firing, but at least they have seen the boys. Oh, how I want to be on the front line! It's so interesting, and at the same time so dangerous, and yet, for some reason, I'm not afraid.

. . .

I remember the days when I took part in the attacks together with Solomatin, Commander of the 2nd Rifle Battalion, *who I loved, but I didn't believe in his love. He did everything for me. But he was facing death and didn't care much who to pay court to, and he was able to do everything, probably because I'm a girl and have been fighting courageously. As soon as I left him, the remarkable regiment commander was killed right beside him, and Nikolay S. started calling the shots in the regiment.*

I went to the front line. And met some guys who were familiar with our girls Shura and Dusya: the battalion commander and his deputy. They made me feel welcome. I fell into the company of a good guy, a senior lieutenant, company commander. He took me under his wing. I went into an attack with him. As I ran through the rye, I saw Blokhin, Commander of the 1st Rifle Battalion, *appear as if out of nowhere. I learned they would go into an offensive that night, and joined him.*

At 3 o'clock in the morning we launched an attack, there was firing all around, and I was at the front of combat formations. Blokhin noticed me and told me to go back. Shapiro, the Jewish political commissar, chased me away. Dawn was breaking. I walked, feeling cold, with having nothing on but my underwear, bra and camouflage cloak. Where are ours? The Fritzes are on three sides. I saw a guard looming in the distance. But whose? Through the rye, I crept closer: our soldiers, an outpost, tired, sleeping in their pits. I ran up to the guard. He was sleeping standing upright. I found out it was Solomatin's battalion. I lay down with the boys under their waterproof capes. In the morning they woke up and wondered how I'd managed to find them. There we were, sitting.

Suddenly a German plane strafed the ground 100 meters away from us. Tairov, the Deputy Commander, said: '*In 10 minutes or so, the enemy will counterattack.*' *And so it happened. We were ordered to take the hill, and we did, I was in the front ranks. I didn't at first see, but then, from behind the mountain, 100 meters away, self-propelled guns appeared with assault forces. I fired at the enemy troops. About 5 meters to my left, an SPG crushed a senior lieutenant, a captain and some soldiers. My rifle jammed. I sat down, sorted it out and started firing again.*

Ten meters ahead, a tank was coming straight at me. I felt for my grenades – but I had lost them while crawling through the rye. I was not scared, I thought I could creep away. About 7 meters away, our 76mm artillery blasted a trench. There were tanks passing by, and grenades were thrown at us from them, and all kinds of firing (machine guns, SMGs, shells). We destroyed 8 tanks, the others retreated. After it was all over, when I saw the dead and wounded, it was terrible. The captain gave me a watch before he died.

We got trophies. I long kept a blue kerchief from the tank as a memory, but it's lost now. Tairov said: 'When the attack began, I remembered about you, and you were ahead, lying there, so I worried very much.' Tairov and Solomatin (who had also come) quarreled. Tairov, an old soldier, had ordered to hold on to the last, or else [the enemy] would surround us by morning, but Solomatin said: 'I am in charge here.' When they went away, I saw General Babayan and hid from him, so as not to get sent to the rear. By nightfall, I went to the command post. All the Lithuanians were taken under guard, because it had turned out that an old peasant woman, who had been ordered to go to the rear, asked if she could get her horse from the meadow first; but when we took the village back from the Fritzes, the woman was found there again.

At night we were surrounded. I and Solomatin were alone, and he hit on me: 'We're gonna die anyway.' I didn't blame him; he is young, and it's his right to think like that. I wasn't afraid to die, but I began to cry, because people say that a girl is always to be blamed for everything, even though the situation is against her and she is forced to do that. I resisted to the last.

Fortunately, two days later another division

liberated us. Solomatin continued to make passes at me […]. *I took my rifle, grenades, and went around in search of a place with room for depressed feelings. There were Germans all around, I had to turn now right, now left. I met artillery guys and they asked where I was going. I told them. 'Come with us,' they said. And I joined them. It was good to be with them. I did long marches with them, sitting on their guns. I got a letter from Blokhin who wrote: 'I'm in charge now, come to me.' We did a march of 60 km. I was tired, because we had to go through the mountains. I lay down and thought I'd run away from the guys when they fell asleep, because they were so good I felt uncomfortable telling them I had to go. They fell asleep, but I was so exhausted I couldn't resist either.*

Somebody shook me awake. I saw two submachine gunners from my training company. I had to go to the rear, orders are orders. But, by mistake, I didn't get there. Near the village of Obukhovo, to the north and further west of it, I was so busy speaking with Blokhin that I turned the wrong way, not where our training company had gone. I found myself in the 136th Regiment surrounding some enemy groups. I spent the night there, and the next morning went to see what was going on. I spotted 30 Fritzes, then ran with the scouts to catch them. There was a fight. Two Germans jumped out of the bushes and killed our captain with their rifle butts. He was just six steps away from us, but the bushes were too thick. We caught and shot both of them.

The Germans split into two groups and ran off in opposite directions. Our boys pursued them, but I had to go "home" to my company. Along the way, I found a wounded soldier. He asked me to search for more wounded men, and crawled away. I moved along. I was too deep in my thoughts and forgot that I was in a dangerous place. Crossing a bridge, I casually looked down at an overgrown gully. And what on earth did I see? A Fritz standing there! I shouted, "Hände hoch!" and up went 6 hands: there were three of them. One mumbled something I did not understand. I only knew how to say the words "quick," "forward," and I shouted out those. They scrambled out of the gully. I took away their weapons, watches, cream, mirrors, etc. When we walked about 1.5 kilometers, I noticed that one of the Germans had only one boot on. That's what he had mumbled in the gully, asking me to let him put on the other boot, but I didn't understand. I met a fellow soldier: "Do you have the time?" I said, "Here." "Show me," he asks. "Take it." And he ran off with the watch. We approached a village. The Fritzes started feeling bold and asked me, "Gut or kaput?" I answered, "Will be gut," and they all turned to look at me. I entered the village (this was in Poland). I was in camouflage, with a Finnish knife, grenades, holding my rifle at the ready, a *real bandit. The village women stared at me. Then they all started inviting me to dinner. So many cheers!*

There I met Sasha Shchekochikhin, Commander of the 120mm mortar battery, *wh*[om] *I liked. I and Kalya Petrova used to go to dine with Blokhin – he would give us milk, etc. And then I fell in love with Sasha and began to feel uncomfortable being treated like that. Sometimes, we'd ask Blokhin to go visit Sasha S. together, saying that he had an accordion and all, while both Kalya and I liked Sasha. Blokhin, knowing this, would reply, "He's busy," even though Sasha wasn't busy and would have been glad if we came. I was the first to declare my love to Sasha in a letter. That's why, when he replied in the affirmative, I felt ashamed and couldn't confirm my love. Oh, how I cried when leaving (after I captured the three Fr*[itzes]*), because I thought he didn't love me while I'd become attached to him, and because I thought it was the last time: either of us could be killed, with the situation being so serious.*

Almost at the same time as I was with Blokhin and others, I was fooling around with Solomatin, but I knew this was only temporary. Now I can't fall in love with anyone. Although I don't believe Solomatin, I dream about meeting with him again, he's a rare kind of man. I'm sure Blokhin is already having a fling in the rear: he had a girl there named Tanya whose letters he didn't allow me to read. I correspond with Grisha, Dima, Kost[ya]*, and*

Nikolay, but just for the fun of it, they're not so close at all, just comrades, even though they are dreaming about something. The guys feel lonely at the front, and I don't want to offend them. After I sent three letters to Dima, I only received one dull short letter from him. I asked him to send all my photos back. 3 years ... We both have had our own experiences, but there's no point writing about those, and we have already written about all the interesting things. How can I explain why I get disappointed in guys so quickly? They cheat, but sometimes I get on their nerves myself and tell them to leave me alone.

I would like to have a female friend. I often wonder about Anna Smirnova and Masha Piskunova, I really like them, but I don't know yet, they're not from our division. Why is it that in this mass of boys I'm always alone? I don't know. Even if you have a man, absences will happen and other unpleasant things. One buddy from the 215th Rifle Division, K., offered me perfume and everything I wished, but no one can buy me like that. I could've fooled him, [but] I don't want to have problems, because he's a high rank.

17 OCTOBER 1944

War. Sasha, Kalya and me spent the night at Vovik Yemelyan[ov]'s, Chief Intelligence Officer in the 3rd Division 5th Army, *but then we got left behind just as accidentally as we'd found him. We broke through the Germ[an] border near the town of Naumiestis, a bit to the left of it. I was invited by some tankmen, they showed me the insides of their tank. What good, tactful guys. Everybody knows me from the newspapers.*

Ever since I was awarded the Order of Glory 3rd Class, back in April, the newspapers wouldn't stop writing about me. Our heroic deeds were announced by the Soviet information Bureau. They said, "A group of girls who graduated from a sniper training school successfully operates in the units of "N" military formation. In the period from April 5th to May 14th, they killed over 300 German soldiers and officers. Private 1st class Roza Shanina killed 15 Nazis, private 1st class Y. Krasnoborova killed 14, privates 1st class L. Tanoylova and V. Smirnova each killed 12."

Then, in an article titled "Sniper Girls", the Red Star Newspaper revealed a short biography of me and described some episodes of my military life, along with a quote. It was what I had said to my sniper girls after one of ours, Maria Schwarz, had been killed: *"Girls, let's take revenge for her, she was so young."* Indeed, she was only twenty when shot by a Nazi sniper.

A Canadian newspaper described me as "the unseen terror of East Prussia."

Then my portrait was printed on the front page of the 5th Army's newspaper "Unichtozhim Vraga" ["We'll Defeat the Enemy"]. Thereafter, every soldier at the front would recognize me.

I met the artillery guys who had seen 5 of our girls get killed at the Neman River. They see that our fate is not easy either. I'm ready to run away to the front line again, I even cry because I'm not allowed to be there. But I want to ... How can I explain it? Some force draws me back there. I'm bored here. Some people are saying I just want to get back to the boys, but I don't have anyone I know there. I want to see real war again. I'm still here because I am a platoon assistant commander, or else I'd have already gone.

. . .

Still no word about my missing brother Fedya. We already lost Misha, my parents' fourth son, to the clutches of war. His death notice reached Mother's hands in the last days of 1941. It said: *Mikhail Yegorovich Shanin, a machine-gunner of the 137th rifle regiment, died a heroic death in the battle at Malaya Vishera on December 22, 1941.*

Mother was inconsolable for months.

18 OCTOBER 1944

*We searched for the RS[1] men, but couldn't find them.
We spent the night with another battery. There were
attacks ... We broke through the border. There we met
Vanya from the 338th* [Rifle Division]. *What a meeting!
But we had to part again. We found our unit, already in
German territory. Prisoners, dead and wounded soldiers
... We attacked a bunker, took 27 prisoners, 14 officers,
but they'd resis*[ted] *hard. I set off "home" to my unit and
came across the div*[ision] *headquarters. I got closer to
the front line and spent the night at Osmak's*—Major in
the 215th Rifle Division. *I like him, but he's very
presumptuous—that's what makes me like him,
probably?*

*I went to see General Kozyryan and the political
dir*[ector]. *I sincerely cried when they would not allow*

me to go to the front line. How can I explain that? Arrived "home" and received a letter from Agniya Butorina. I always remember her as a good friend of mine from grades 5-7. She writes that her life is fractured and she feels bored. I believe her: how can a girl live a normal life with no boys around? It will be the same after the war, too. Seems like I'm going to be sent to the rear, but I dream about escaping to the front line.

Agniya Butorina, Roza's classmate:

My dear friend Roza... she was the only girl in the 7th grade who attended shooting classes and had a Young Sharpshooter badge as a person who had reached qualifying standards. I remember that well. And her heart ... it seems that even in the midst of war, she thought about me and understood my uncomplicated life and struggles. There she was, fighting the enemy and ever in danger of being killed, and I complained of how bored I was. I feel somewhat embarrassed now.

---

1. Probably the Katyusha operators; The Katyusha was a multiple rocket launcher.

20 OCTOBER 1944

It was only yesterday that I ran away to the front line. There was an attack, but now we stay here, entrenched. Rain, mud and cold. The nights are long. We're going to push forward.

I just hope I won't be reprimanded for taking part in fights without permission. But, goaded by my eternal boredom, I more and more often run to the front line and fight like any other soldier. Oh God! How much I hate this Soviet policy that keeps women off the front unless absolutely necessary!

It is the same persisting boredom that makes my thoughts wander—especially during the nights I have to be on the watch. I remember my short leave the past September. I was so happy to return to Arkhangelsk for a few days and again see my friends. *On the train on my way there, I often caught people smiling slyly as they spied my decorations.*

It was such a rewarding welcomed leave. I felt charged by meeting M. Makarova, a teacher from the Arkhangelsk Pedagogical College where I studied, as well as my dear children from the kindergarten. How impressed they were by my front stories!

M. Makarova:

My relations with her [Roza] were somewhat different from those that can normally be expected between a teacher and students. She was my friend, and I loved her very much. I lived badly during the war. When Roza was on a leave, she dropped by. When she saw me, she dashed out and came back with two loaves of bread and some canned food. Such a gesture mattered a lot back then. She was always generous, kind and warmhearted. Even if she hadn't done anything heroic, I would have remembered her all my life anyway.

The three days that she spent with us passed too quickly. The children listened to her stories about the front life with breathless attention, and we adults were no less attentive too. She told us a lot about her comrades-in-arms and what it was like fighting shoulder to shoulder with them, and very little about herself. When she was leaving, all of our kindergarten staff together with the children went out to see her off. Marching smartly, with her rucksack on her back, she went away, sometimes looking back and waving at us.

24 OCTOBER 1944

There were no conditions to write: I had to fight and march with the others. A lot of wounded and killed men. I was summoned by the regiment commander. Oh God, how much gossip. I remember crying in the battalion, offended by someone telling a bad joke in my presence; I found it disrespectful. I remember my comrades who fell during that period. Why, I could have shared the same fate, and this is the thanks I get!

Even my fellow girls looked at me ironically when we met. The world is filled with lies. It seems I don't have the strength to look at this lying world all my life. I got 8 letters from Yashka Gudkov. Just to be courteous, I responded with one small letter, because he does everything for me. I'm waiting for the photos, and when

I get them I won't write back anymore. Yashka understands army girls properly.

25 OCTOBER 1944

After all, it's nice to have [at] *least some kind of female friend. Sasha, sometimes I have fun with you. I share everything with you. I was summoned by Colonel Novozhilov,* Chief Political Officer in the 215th Rifle Division of the 5th Army, *regarding my letter in which I asked to be sent to the front line and criticized our officers.*

28 OCTOBER 1944

Battle of Pillkallen[1]. The city was taken with our soldiers, all of them were killed. Only one man from the Shtrafbat company returned alive, unharmed, all the rest died.

I myself fought for a village near Pillkallen. We took it many times and were expelled again. I was very successful fighting back one of the enemy's counterattacks. 15 kills for sure, as I was at close range and shot a lot. Four of our artillerymen watched through ten-fold and six[-fold] binoculars. When the Fritzes started to crawl, we could only see their helmets, and I shot at them. The bullets were ricocheting off their helmets, which we could see very well because I used tracer cartridges. First they were at a distance of 200

meters, then they stood up to full heigh[t] 100 meters
out. When they got within 20 meters, we fled. We had
been behind an embankment by a wood side, so we
escaped easily. We retreated to the cottage, but the other
"Slavs" had all fled. We were left alone. Beside me,
Captain Aseyev was killed (he was the artillery
div[ision] commander, a Hero of the Sov[iet] Union).
And we were the last to retreat.

We were ordered to reestablish the position. We crept
back and took the cottage again, expelling the Fritzes.
Then I went to the Regimental Command post, tired,
and ate for the first time that day. It was 12 P.M., so I fell
sound asleep.

Suddenly, the basement was fired at from a very close
distance. Fritzes, 15 of them, had crept close to the
cottage. They were destroyed by the artillerymen w[ho]
had heard them shooting, being in a barn near the
cottage. The girls were all cowards and fled. Only
Kaleriya was brave. The other girls, seeing the danger,
were about to tear me to pieces because I led them into
the battle. This time Sasha Koreneva was killed and two
were wounded: Valya Lazarenko and Anna
Kuz[netsova]. I'm afraid to go "home," as the girls put
all the blame on me. Soldiers and commanders are
pleased with my bravery. When they heard about it in

the Corps, I was recommended for the Ord[er] *of Glory 1st* [Class] *for repelling those attacks.*

Before being sent off, I was allowed to read it. My eyes filled with tears on seeing the recognition of my bravery. The recommendation read like this:

> "Senior Sergeant Shanina, during a breakthrough deep into the enemy defenses on the border of East Prussia during the invasion of East Prussia, took an active part in the battles in support of the advance infantry, fired flawlessly to eliminate Nazi soldiers and officers.
>
> During a German counterattack on 10/26/44, as part of the 707th Infantry Regiment, under the city of Pillkallen, Comrade Shanina showed exemplary courage and boldness, with her presence, as a girl, showing the soul of a true fighter of endurance and courage, driving skilful fire on the Nazis. To her credit, Comrade Shanina has killed 59 Fritzes.
>
> For their courage and bravery shown in the battles of the invasion of East Prussia, Comrade Shanina is worthy of the medal 'For Courage.'"

Tears were already obstructing my view, and setting aside the guilt with which the girls' wrath plagued me, I remembered why I was at the front. I remembered the true purpose of the war I was fighting. And it wasn't to make girlfriends or find love, but to kill as many Nazis as I could. To protect the Motherland, like the true daughter that I was.

---

1. Now Dobrovolsk, a rural settlement in the Krasnoznamensk Urban District of the Kaliningrad Region.

5 NOVEMBER 1944

I haven't written anything for a long while, there was no time, I was on the front line. I went with the girls to Voviks. Some tongues wagged that Cap[tain] Aseyev had died because of me, while I myself had nearly been killed because of him. He was drunk and wouldn't retreat, although we had to, at least for a while, because the [situation] required us to do so. So we insisted. I really liked Nikolay Shevchenko, lieut[enant] in the artillery, brother of the pilot Shevchenko, who is a Hero of the Soviet Union. He is in love with me, and he doesn't care about being not very tall, but I don't like [anyone] who's even a little shorter than me. And still I have a soft spot for him.

I spent the night with Nikolay Fyodorov, Captain, Deputy Commander in the 3rd Rifle Batalion. *Good guy. He dotes on me: gets me anything I want (suit, hat, gifts). But I don't love him. Ah, my enigmatic nature. I deceive him, taking his gifts when I don't love him. "An Enigmatic Nature" by Chekhov.*

The celebration is right around the corner. Invitations ... We made a schedule starting from the 5th to ... But alas, November 6-7 are working days for us, so we couldn't do some of the things we'd planned to do. We spent the evening before November 6 with some Katyusha boys. Tankers arrived, and Vovka Klokov, the Guards Major, too. I wanted to go to Borovik to spend the holiday with him, but we have to work on these days. The Katyusha boys are good guys after all. It's just that I love Vovka Leipson, the Medical Service Guards Lieutenant, like a dear little brother of mine, but he hints at something, and I don't like it. He gave me a Finnish knife. I don't understand anything at all, even life itself, it's all so devious.

7 NOVEMBER 1944

We met the morning of the 7th on the front line, while the evening of the 6th was spent with Nikolay Fyodorov; we had fun, but there was something unexpected, too. A photographer came from Moscow. The generals called me, as a repres[entative] of the girls, a front-line sniper. But Nikolay didn't want me to leave and told them I wasn't there. On the morning of the 7th I met with the generals, and they scolded me for not coming. I said I hadn't been informed.

"Home". I got invitat[ions] from the guys calling me "sugar," and "sweetheart," and hell... I decided not to go anywhere because I was dirty and tired. Suddenly, an invitation from Molchanov, Lieutenant Colonel, Executive Editor of the 5th Army "Unichtozhim Vraga" ("We'll Defeat the Enemy") newspaper. *I*

couldn't refuse. They're very good comrades of mine and might think I'd gone elsewhere. I was coughing, but I went to them anyway. I arrived there and fell ill, so I lay in bed for two nights and the 7th. So, half of the 7th in Germany, half in Lithuania or the USSR.

I returned "home," got a bunch of letters, but none pleased me. I worry about Nikolay. He disgusts me even more, because he acted very badly on the 6th: he wanted to get me drunk and take advantage of me. I can't stand it. I'm sick of Yashka's letters; he's stupid, I didn't understand his nature before and thought he was a good guy. I only occasionally respond to his letters, only to get the photo from him.

11 NOVEMBER 1944

I was summoned by General Kozyryan. He criticized us for poor discipline, roaming around, being absent. During the holidays there were no absences at all. In fact, they hadn't done anything for us in the division, but we had to celebrate the holidays somehow anyway. What can we do, when the "tops" don't work with us? Our squad is working normally [...]. It was muddy outside when I came home, and I saw Nik[olay] F. there. He'd come to apologize for his bad behavior, but there were a lot of people around, and he said nothing, looking very sad.

I received letters from the preschools in Moscow and Arkhangelsk. They are all proud of my achievements. Yes, my portrait was in the "Humor" magazine on

November 7. But I am too overrated. I do only what is required of every Soviet soldier, that's all. I am famous everywhere, it's too much.

14 NOVEMBER 1944

There are some people here fighting with me, who I respect and admire more than others.

1. Captain Tishin ...

2. Captain Vovka Stepanenko ...

3. Captain Pavel Blokhin ...

4. Senior Sergean[t] *Mishka Ponarin 2*

5. Senior L[ieutenan]*t Nikolay Solomatin ...*

6. Senior L[ieutenan]*t Nikolay, artilleryman, 184th R.D.,* [2]*97th* [R.]*R., 1st b*[attalio]*n.*

7. Major Asmak 3-4

8. Lieutenant Vovka Leipson 3

9. Colonel Khoroshov 3

10. Captain Nokolay Fyodorov ...

11. ... Sen[ior] *L*[ieutenan]*t Borovik.*

. . .

[I re]*alize that I have earned honor in the army* – [at] *the front, that's OK, but why spread it out over the whole Soviet* [Un]*ion? I* [haven']*t done as much* [as] *they say I have. Going* [to] *bed. A lot of guys are eager to see Roza* [Sh]*anina, how can it be explained ...?* [The]*y picture me as a beau*[ty] *or a hero? I don't* [un]*derstand.*

? NOVEMBER 1944

THE EXACT DATE IS UNKNOWN DUE TO THE DAMAGED
EDGE OF THE PAGE

Oh, what happened today! At night we went to the 277th R.D. [I m]et with Captain Lyosha, handsome, but [behaves] like an idiot, who does he think we are? We were invited by a guy from Arkhangelsk, a food supply officer. [...] taught him a lesson as to what snipers are, [...] spent the night with Toska and left in the morning.

We moved over to the 618th Regiment, but settled in not too well, [...] get normalized, I and Kalya went [to] the administrative platoon of the 711th to visit Nikolay there, and what did we see ["...] nothing" in the gully. I spent the night at Nikolay's, [...] pilot Yasha arrived. I can [not st]and him, he's stupid, [una]ble to string a sentence together, I saw him off quickly. If it weren't for [...] wouldn't speak with him at all. [...] at Nikolay's, he's madly [in love] with me, that's for sure, his letters conf[irm] *everything. Then I visited Major Grunichev, I like him and his guys really much (tactful, modest); there's only one son-of-a-bitch among them, Vovka Ivanov, while here all the guys are darlings.*

In the evening, there was a conversation about Stalin's report. I didn't manage to get to Grunichev, even though he'd invited me so earnestly. I was also invited by the commander of the 711th Rifle Regiment, and, quite unexpectedly, found myself [at] Colonel's, the ch[ief] of the division headquarters. Time was well spent; I was three-sheets to the wind, but even being that drunk I was able to teach them that we were not what they expected. They were offended and even insulted by my words. In the morning I got in a jalopy and left, summoned by the junior platoon commander. Today I hope to visit Grunichev. I'm writing this while with the artillery boys of the 2nd division; they're not bad at all.

18 NOVEMBER 1944

My mood is nasty, why? I was just now at Nikolay's, spending the night there, that's where I began to feel somewhat out of sorts. I met a boy in the artillery. What a boy, I liked him a great deal, extremely handsome and shy, but alas! Nikolay is close by.

I thought about my entire relationship with Nikolay. I respect him very little, but still respect him anyway. All the girls like him, but this, I think, is only as long as they are just comrades, until he starts making passes at them – take Sasha Yekimova, for example. I'm an unlucky person. After all, I made friend[s] with him just impulsively, not as I would wish. I remember the first day I met him on the offensive, when I "ran away" to the front line. Tall, dirty, stained with mud and clay, in a long overcoat, like a true warrior. I respect him for his bravery; he is a real Soviet soldier, but he doesn't shine in upbringing or education – simple guy, a gunner. I remember the first days spent with Nikolay. Why didn't I have the courage to reject him? The circumstances: cold and mud, I was undressed and needed help, and he did help me – in short, it was impossible to do otherwise. And now I like him a little bit; other than that I force myself, pushing into my mind that I respect him and that I miss him when I haven't seen him for a while. Why do I force into my mind that I even love him? Because after Blokhin I wasn't able to respect anyone, and I don't want to be alone, I want to have a friend, what else? Ch... I now make friends with him, but I can't explain why, although I understand but just can't explain. It's not a part of his character to live with style. All his things and presents are rags and garbage, but he gives you those from the heart (a suit, a kerchief, a hat). He has no masculinity; he messes about with some girlish scenery postcards, and there is another gunner just like him, too. This is not a man: a doormat. I love warriors. He fights well, but doesn't look like a Russian warrior; he's like a girl, and I hate that.

Now I and the girls are being bored. Tomorrow is the Artillery Day. A secret commission has come to monitor the girls' behavior – I know. Oh, this army life, they all think we're a bunch of prostitutes, and it's so offensive for a modest girl to see all this.

. . .

And Nikolay suggests we should get married, but formally, with documents, to make it easier to live together. No, I don't think about marriage; even just in the documents, it would only make more gossip.

How does Nikolay confess his love? It's impossible even for me, but if a man falls at the feet of a girl, he can well be called a "doormat". I still don't understand whether it's true or he's just a hypocrite.

We're singing a song with the girls:

> *"They despise our soldier's uniform,*
>   *they never leave us alone, and they*
>   *never hesitate to call us prostitutes."*

It is a rephrased verse from the folk song "The Candle Is Burning Down In The Cabin":

> "They despise his sailor's uniform, they
>   never leave him alone, and they
>   never hesitate to call the sailor a
>   drunkard."

The idea was to put us in a better mood, but *everyone's crying, that's the mood here.*

. . .

Tomorrow is the Artillery Day; where shall I go in the evening? And will I actually go anywhere? So hard! Oh my God! The results on the front line were poor, and nothing else pleases me now. The Fritzes wander too far away; it's not easy to shoot them. Today I'm gonna write down something about I. ...

Dear mother, although you don't miss me too much, I am bored, having nothing to be pleased with, and I really want to be with you. Oh, it kind of seems that I should commit suicide, this is my future, yes, there's no other way. I got [a letter] from Yashka, he'd only been with me for 10 minutes back then, and that short time was enough to spread gossip about me and Captain Aseyev. No rest for him, even in the afterlife, that poor fellow.

Oh yes, I received a Certificate of Merit from the Young Communist League. I wrote a letter to a girl – a stranger – who, like me, is eager to be in the fire of war. She's a medic; I told her everything. Yesterday I praised the guys from the 2nd division, today I say they are bastards – indeed, you can never be sure of what's going on in someone else's mind.

20 NOVEMBER 1944

I had so many invitations for yesterday's evening party from many people (Katyusha guys, Commander of the 711th Reg., Grunichev, scouts, guys from the 120th Battery, and many more), but I decided to reject all of them and go spend the evening with Nikolay, even though I knew I would spend it most ~~poorly~~[1] modestly, because it was on the front line and nearly in the trenches.

I didn't go anywhere until dark, and after dark went to Nikolay and quarrelled with him about Lena – my rival from the medical battalion. Finally, I found myself with the artillery guys and, as the saying goes, could not suddenly go against my heart. Since I am so crazy about Nikolay Shevchenko, I had it out with him behind Nikolay F.'s dugout with bullets whistling around us.

Later I wrote him a letter, like: "But I'm given to the one and will love no other one ..." I wrote something for the guys in their album, and for N[ikolay] Sh[evchenko] I wrote: "Know that my love will follow you through the misty fields ..." Oh, how I liked him, but N.F. wouldn't leave until I left the party and N.Sh. wanted to see me off, and there was shooting like in a duel. Then I made up with N.F. for he was so persistent. In the morning I came home, having said a few words regarding my Finnish knife: "Don't hurt my feelings. Mishka Ponarin was my first love, not only at the front but in my life, and he died."

I am at the artillery major's; I like him as a person, he's modest and kind. And Nikolay Shevchenko is just like a kid. He immediately fell madly in love with me, and he even raved in his sleep, even though he's a lieutenant, chief of artillery reconnaissance. It was the first time I so cruelly played on the nerves of these guys – the two Nikolays and some others, and it was the first time they were so persistent following me and even had a duel because of me. And where? On the front line.

---

1. The word was crossed in the diary.

23 NOVEMBER 1944

Oh, God, so much to write down. Yesterday Sasha put a handsome boy from Commander Dovgal's company on her post as a sentry, while she went aside to do her doings in a ditch. What a shame. Shame because as Sasha left her post, I, as Platoon Assistant Commander, was held responsible for her misbehavior. *But how could it be helped if she had to relieve herself? Today, no, yesterday she reported that she was called to a seminar, but she wasn't there, having a date with another guy who had come to visit her. Using formalities for the sheer sake of appearance, she and others lie every now and again, so why should we think we are good girls and the guys wouldn't lie to us, too? I explained to Nikolay Shevchenko that I can't be with him, and he is with Sasha now, while he asked me not to let him down. I never did. Let him be happy if he can. Oh, it's so hard.*

. . .

Oh, God, I remember the day when we were invited by General Kozyryan to spend the evening with him, but we weren't home, being on a visit to some guys we weren't familiar with. And one of our girls was raped, which was not her fault: "My life is broken, I am no longer a girl" – those are her words. If only it were someone she loved, not someone she was hardly familiar with! And she had fought off so many male attacks! At the gates of my sanctuary there have been more than one enemy, too, but successfully repelled. Can something like this really happen to us? Yes, and we need to be afraid. [...].

I went to the auto guys, they welcomed me and called Nikolay Borovik, who I liked terribly, and now he confessed his love, too. I don't know to what extent he is being sincere, but this is how it seems to me. He's not eloquent, and I don't like that. That trait is a must, but how fully it's developed is not a big deal.

The Katyusha guys came yesterday in the evening, they gave me a little ride, but I jumped out of the cab and ran away, crying for a long while. I walked 15 kilometers and reached the front line, got lost because it was pitch dark, so I had to grope my way, crying. Why? I don't like this life on the road. It's wartime, and we have to work at the front, paying little attention to any other things, and what are we doing now?

. . .

I sobbed my heart out all the way, because I was so sad. I was alone at night, there were only bullets whistling and fires burning. I came back, went to bed and slept from 1 1 at n[ight] until 2 p.m. the next day.

Today I wrote some letters and explained a few things to Nikolay F. I received letters from Lukyanenko and some other tankers. They all know me and remember how I laughed mischievously as I sang "The Germans stamped, darning their uniforms," and they have all seen my photo in the "Crocodile" magazine, but I haven't seen it. My pictures from newspapers and magazines are kept in the guys' cases or hung on the walls. It seems there are more people who respect me than those who hate me. And as for those who hate me, that's because I won't give them what they want, or because I was rude to them, or because they're jealous. Oh, how many dirty things were told to Yashka Gudkov when he visited. It seems we'll be transferred to another division.

24 NOVEMBER 1944

When I learned about our transfer, I went to spend the night with Nikolay, not because I'm sad to be leaving him but because there were some things I needed to collect: a waterproof cape, a book and a watch. But I didn't take the watch. I'm more sorry for Nikolay Shevchenko. Now I don't want to see Nikolay F. at all.

The girls are not home. 10 people in different divisions, I blushed for them a lot.

[We're leaving] to the 203rd Reserve Regiment. Now again I have no one; I am on my own. I don't care a damn about Nikolay F.; Nikolay Shevchenko is no match for me, it seems: he's short, even though

handsome. No chance to meet Nikolay Borovik again – he's fighting south-west of the city of Naumiestis.

We came to the rear of the division and now we're spending the night in the training company. We settled well – after all, profitable connections are better than the People's Commissariat. I met the General's entourage, had dinner, now I'm in a devilish mood. There's an accordion playing, we're like in apartments. Just a bit further away from the frontline, but everything feels so different, as if the place is located in the country's hinterland, it's so good. Somehow a girl is always welcomed pretty well: "Come here, join us ..." Oh, God, it's so boring, so very, very boring, how can it be explained? Still, it's better to be with at least some kind of friends; more fun with them. I find myself longing to be with my old friends, especially Nikolay Shevchenko or Borovik (I'd prefer Shevchenko though). I could also visit Fyodorov – or, well, perhaps, not yet.

26 NOVEMBER 1944

We settled in the 203rd Reserve Regiment; not bad, resting today.

27 NOVEMBER 1944

We washed in the bath, and there was an incident: a bunch of naked men were let in as we were still inside, naked, so we screamed bloody murder! For the first time I saw German Fraus, and I didn't like them.

Yesterday there was dancing. I'm not a good dancer, but I was impressed that they care about people after all. We wanted to go visit the auto guys. Vovka came – but I couldn't see him, I wasn't allowed to. I was watched, mostly out of jealousy.

As we walked from the bath, we recalled how the Germans captured our girls. Dusya Kekesheva saw everything. She fought herself free, while Shambarova played dead. Are the other two still alive somewhere?

They're in the hands of their executioners. Here now are German women to take revenge on, but my heart is too cold to care about it. I'm cold-blooded about anything. Strange enough, but I can tell it straightly that I am now able to kill not only Germans, but anyone I am ordered to. I can't be otherwise; I've gotten used to such a life, and I get in a bad mood if everything is quiet around. I crave war – that's what brings happiness to my life now, but how can I fulfil it?

[...]

The following fragment in Roza's diary is written in a different handwriting.

It was June of 1947.

It was a beautiful, sunny day. The capital of the Soviet Union, Moscow, was back to its former bustling life. Two years have passed since the end of the severe war. Soldiers have returned home. The doors of secondary schools, tech colleges and institutes opened before them again. How these people have changed after two years of peaceful life. Today the streets of Moscow were especially noisy: it was Sunday. Two girls were walking along Gorky Street. Each had a bundle in her hand. They were obviously in a hurry. When they reached a white house, they stopped at the entrance. After a few minutes a third girl came out. Her face was bright with a smile. In no more than a few seconds the trio continued their walk. They started to dispute about something, accompanying their words with gestures. Each of them held her ground not willing to give up. Finally, the dispute ended. Exhausted from the heat, they slowed their steps. There was silence. They saw a couple walking towards them. The girls did not take their eyes off the couple: a slender, elegantly dressed young man in uniform; in his hands he had a baby wrapped in a thin blanket. Walking beside him was a slim girl with brunette hair. They were cheerfully chatting about something. Looking at them, one could tell they were happy. The young man turned his gaze to the three girls. Their eyes met. In an instant, all their front life flashed before their mind's eye. They recalled the friendship between the sniper girls and the Katyusha boys.

As they came close to each other, they did not stop. They just nodded their heads in greeting. Two years of peace had changed these people so much. It was difficult to recognize them. The girls were college students, while the young man studied at the academy and had a wife and a son. It was the first time they met after the war. In two years, the whole relationship had changed. Once they were great friends. So why didn't this young man and these three girls stop, why didn't they recollect the hard times – the war and all the hardships and sorrows shared together? They were so far from it now. The young man had apparently considered it improper to admit he had been their friends because his wife was here with him. The three girls continued on their way, but now they were silent. If you looked at their faces, you would easily see that one of them was very gloomy. She had been obviously hurt by this meeting. This is how a good front-line friendship ends.

Dear Rozka, I had this dream on the night of November ?, 1944.
    A. Yekimova.
    Rozka!

If we stay alive and healthy, but scatter to different regions, I beg you – do not forget me and Kalyushka, our brave roaming trio.

29 NOVEMBER 1944

As she wrote down this dream, Sasha Y[ekimova] read my diary. It made us both sour. Yes, she has now become really dear to me, like never before, because, after all, we are fellow soldiers and share everything, sorrow and joy. Nobody is perfect, and I don't blame her for that negative trait I noted earlier.

I feel terrible.

I've visited the newspaper office again, what with being 7 km away from it. We wanted to leave, but couldn't, so we'll wait till tomorrow. Music! The radio is playing the nicest things. I poured my heart out to Agniya Butorina, telling her that I don't even dream about seeing anyone, because there is something new happening every single minute. And the world? A mess all around [...]. Many are already no longer girls; I do not blame them, but they conduct themselves with dignity, like Tonya P. She became a woman when she was civilian, but she hardly allows herself anything disgraceful at the front. But most of them are still girls.

There was a concert yesterday, and there were handsome boys, like babies, dancing very well. And that whore A[...], although pretty, is really neglectful, which can be seen simply by looking at her. And who she's messing with! The Supply Ch[ief] – of course, to enrich herself, I don't think she loves such a penguin.

I remember two guys who I don't know well enough: Nikolay Borovik, he's not so close a friend and less memorable than Nikolay Shevchenko, although the latter is not a match for me, such a child. And I don't write to them; if I do write to someone, that's only for the sake of writing, and I don't dream about them at all.

In fact, I haven't figured out my future, but there are many options: 1) entering an institute; 2) if that doesn't work out, then, maybe, social service; I'll give myself fully to the education of orphans, since I specialize in teaching presc[hool]; 3) I'll most likely kill myself when I learn the fate of the country and some of my family and friends. For the moment, I'd still need to learn a few things, become thoroughly qualified. In fact, I haven't really thought much about my future; just wondered occasionally.

I wanted to train in communications, [learn] Morse code, etc. There are communication courses conducted right next door, but we're leaving soon. I want to have a lot of different specialties, even if I don't use them, just to be qualified, in case they could come in handy. Well, time to finish dreaming, I've had enough for today.

2 DECEMBER 1944

Oh God, I felt so bored. I came to the quartermaster supply depot, and while I was waiting there I remembered everything, everything. Generally, there are two pictures before my eyes:

1) Pavel Blokhin, lying in a dugout in the [11]36th regiment of the 338th [R.]D. near Vitebsk, with a receiver in his hand, shouting into it, trying not to cuss: "Oh, you bloody such-and-such." I sit next to him, and he hangs up and smiles at me.

2) I'm with Nikolay Solomatin, running by the Neman in the woods, on the riverbank, through the bushes, running quickly. I touch my head and find there is no kerchief – my green camouflage kerchief is gone. The day is hot and sunny. I keep running. Nikolay looks at me having a hard time climbing a steep slope; he takes me by the hand and helps me climb up, then kisses me, and we run on. I get stuck on a bush and tear my camouflage, and I only have panties and a bra on underneath, so I ask for a needle and thread, sew it up, and we keep running. We reach a very high bank of the Neman: there is a field to the left, and a forest far in the distance, the river is to the right, with a meadow and woods behind it. We go on quietly, looking at each other from time to time, when suddenly we hear a machine gun stuttering to our left – it is a Fritz. Quickly, we jump down the riverbank and into the bushes, and then we go on through the bushes.

I remember that night when I went with Nikolay to some village where the Germans were. We went through the woods all night, led by a Lithuanian. Going along the r[iver] ..., we went around the forest and came to a tall hill where a farmstead was. We lay down under the bushes on a camouflage cape to have some rest, then stood up, warmed coffee, boiled a couple of chickens and ate ... I don't even remember which direction we went after that ... well, I remember going around the village and having a heavy fight, but I don't remember any more.

. . .

I remember the big march, the rain, I didn't even have an undershirt on; I was soaked to the skin. He brought me a wool dress uniform, but I didn't take it – I only took a cape. We got a bit soaked in the night, finding ourselves in a puddle because it rained so hard. We spent the night together in a horse-cart. I liked him very much; now I'm singing a song: "Where are you honey, where, where are you, where are you, wherever the war took you ... ?"

I'm so bored! An accordion is playing in the workshop. I feel dreadful. I want to be back there now, attacking! Where the fighting is fiercest, that's all I want. And why the hell not? Oh, how irresponsible the top brass are! Enough writing.

3 DECEMBER 1944

I lost Nik[olay] Shevchenko's address. Oh, how sad I am about it – why, I've mechanically eliminated the one whose memory still warmed me. His hat often reminds me of him. A good guy. Oh, how depressed I feel, how sorry I am about losing N. Shevchenko's address. There's marvelous music playing, and my heart sinks at the thought of it all. I've torn up the letter, which I wrote to him and couldn't send without an address. My heart yearns for a caress. There are no boys among those I know who I respect, not even on the horizon, save for maybe N. Borovik, but that is still up in the air. I've torn up the letter I wrote to him.

I sit with Captain Sokol; Captain, propagandist in the 297th Rifle Regiment of the 184th Rifle Division, *once again holding the hope that I can get in to the 338th Infantry Division, though today I've been kicked out by the colonel, the battalion commander and the company commander, so much have I annoyed them with this matter.*

4 DECEMBER 1944

We were on a visit to Major and Captain (Battalion Commander) with Chief of Staff. M[ajo]r Lyashenko, Commander of the 1st Rifle Battalion of the 203rd Reserve Rifle Regiment of the 5th Army. Actually, we're not indifferent to Sasha and those guys. We stayed there from 6 to 11 and missed dancing. They offered us to spend the night with them, but we wouldn't, as this would be ugly, and today I'm regretting we didn't stay, for that was the last evening. After playing some good music we just waved goodbye to each other, without even shaking hands before leaving, as there were a lot of commanders around.

Today 20 km march, mud, wind with snow. We met the Katyusha guys and left with them for the night, although the platoon commander wouldn't allow us. But there is no food there, and no sleep. Sasha and Kalya went to the observation point where Vovka was, and I stayed with Sashka, Chief of Staff; they're modest boys. Too bad we have to move around all the time, there's no way to have a boyfriend, and we're too used to it already and can't do without traveling.

6 DECEMBER 1944

*Oh, Lord! Will you really not come to my aid to make sense of all this? Everything is such a mess. Oh, God! I'll remember the 5th of December for a long time. I came back from the guys. Valka Moshchenko—*the sniper in the female sniper individual platoon of the 184th Rifle Division—*met me, spoiling for a fight, because I had scolded them harshly as they deserved it. Supporting her were Shura Polygalova, Dusya Krasnoborova, Anya Smirnova, Dusya Kekesheva, and she was also silently supported by Zina Shmelyova, Zoya and Masha Rozhkova. They wanted to disgrace and blemish me in front of the platoon and even others. They called me a "heroine" with irony. They attacked me for going AWOL, but this was only an excuse, and the real reason is that I have authority and everybody asks about me. They decided to deprive me of this. Valya even said that I am now nothing to them. This, of course, will not be;*

the girls today are even more attentive to me, they're sorry for me, and they call Valya a fishwife. I am not so low to mess with them, and I'm scolding myself for sinking to talking to them trying to stand my ground.

There were offenses, but I survived, and this, it seems, will be a breaking point in my work. They blame me for being with Molchanov for no reason. Those guys are good comrades, [but] they call us lovers, call me a suck-up – but this nasty trait is not part of my personality. I decided not to go anywhere, but mark any absences, especially if the absent person is among those who accuse me of not working as a platoon assistant commander, while not obeying me in the first place. I didn't boss about, but [they] didn't even listen to me when they should have, and now I will check their work in the trenches. In short, I will report every problem to the quarter and ask to take measures; that will help them feel what it means to be at odds with the platoon commander. And I have never reported on them before, even though they caused a lot of trouble. And they tell me: "You are a platoon assistant commander, it's improper for you to go AWOL," – why, am I not a young girl? After all, I don't do what they do, like Zoyka for example, [...] – but she, too, began to lecture me. I thank them for the knowledge. I am pleased and satisfied that they let me know how a platoon assistant commander should behave, and I'll let them know that smearing a person for no reason can turn out badly. Now I'm gonna kick them around for no reason, too. I'll take the pains, and they won't do what they shouldn't.

. . .

Kaleriya wrote in a letter to her sister that she does all the nasty things which people attribute to us army girls. She lied; she's a modest girl, but was upset and decided to vent her anger by lying to her sister about herself to spite everybody. We broke up with Sasha.

I wrote 30 letters to all corners, some of them businesslike, some of them simple. Today I didn't sleep the whole night. Only a little in the evening, then I woke up and kept thinking about life, about all the girls, about what's right and wrong.

You know, throughout my life at the front there was not a moment when I didn't long for a fight; I want a fierce fight, want to go with the soldiers. I wish I was born a boy – then no one would have paid any attention to me, no one would have felt sorry for me, and I would have fought with all my heart. Now I brought up the issue: I said, "I want to go on the attack," and Kalya and Yeva, who know my nature, believed me, while all the others were like, "Cut the crap!" But Yeva told the girls that she'd heard from the soldiers I had lain under a German tank. And she said she believed me, for I had acted voluntarily then, too.

. . .

I'd give anything to go and fight with the soldiers now. Oh Lord, why do I have this mysterious nature? I just can't understand, but I really crave, crave a fight, a fierce fight. I will give everything, even my life, only to satisfy this urge. It torments me, I can't sleep.

I'll write about the platoon. Alkhimova says, "I don't believe Roza has killed as many Fritzes as she gets credit for."

Let me explain. When we have to defend, I sometimes shoot at a lot of targets, but it's hard to tell if it's a kill or not. Logically, back at school I always hit training targets accurately, and I hit a standing Fritz more often than I miss. And in most cases, I shoot at stationary targets or slowly moving soldiers, for those who run are hard to hit, you'd only scare them. Sometimes I don't have them scored at all, sometimes the score is very rough, sometimes it's undue, but I have no falsely killed Fritzes to my account. If one time I have a kill scored for no reason, the other time a real kill is not scored, and sometimes the score is just made blindly.

I remember I was in the offensive. I can say from the heart, sincerely: in fighting each counterattack I spent 70 rounds or so. In the attack I was against 13 tanks; at 3 of them I didn't shoot, but in 9 I killed everyone. One of them escaped with its driver, but the others were shot up, and their crew members killed or wounded, which couldn't be done only by the bullets of the soldiers who use Berdan rifles – those are dirty, haven't been sighted in for a year and can't guarantee accurate shooting. And I fired at the distance from 50 to just 7 meters. I killed and wounded at least 20. In attacks I often had to shoot at close range, and I surely didn't miss.

I remember the last counterattack: my bullets hit the enemy right in the helmets. There were only heads visible, but the tracer bullets couldn't break through the helmets at 100 meters. We could clearly see them ricocheting and going up in the sky. That's when the guys became assured I shot accurately. I mean, I handled the weapon, and the five of them watched and said, "Well done." I hit standing targets at a distance of 20 meters and clearly killed at least 15, maybe more. So I went hunting twice and was lucky enough to kill 35 Fritzes, because a sniper shoots accurately.

And on defense I often shot from 50 meter[s] at standing targets, hitting them in the chest. My score is 57 Fritzes, and not one of them is a fake kill. Let them talk, I know it's Sasha Yekimova who's behind it all. A person cannot be without negative traits; I don't blame her, it's how she was raised. She's accustomed to care about herself and nobody else. But she has started to change a bit. I got used to her; I'm attached to her and Kalya, I'm bored without them. I respect them more than anyone else in the platoon, and life is always easier when you have friends. All three of us are from different families, each having one year of college background, and all are slightly different personalities because each had her own foundation. But we have something in common anyway, we are friends, and our friendship is firm enough.

Kaleriya Petrova is also my friend. She is a good person, completely free of egotism and brave. She has a lot of common sense, gets to the bottom of everything. She's got an amazing memory, but is just a bit lazy. Sasha, Kalya and me – that's our close-knit roaming trio.

All the girls are more or less pleasant, no beauties or monsters. I like Sasha and Masha most of all; they are not beautiful, but attractive. Only Nyuska is somewhat old-fashioned. Lyolya was born in '22, and Nyusya in '23, the rest in '24 or '25. That's our squad.

I've been writing all day. I'm tired; I will leave it and finish it later. I have been writing letters and my diary all the time, on my lap, leaning up against a wall, and now my back and arm are tired.

7 DECEMBER 1944

I went to the bath, sighted in my rifle, and the platoon sighted [in] theirs, and the day was over.

I wrote Comrade Stalin a letter that I want to be transferred to the battalion. I want to be on the offensive.
    [...].
    We have 15 girls in all. Five, I know for sure, became women as civilians, and seven others, it seems, during the war. As if they couldn't help sinking to it. I went out with boys, because I had done so as a civilian. In 8 m[onth]s, four guys kissed me, and not without reason, because I was well familiar with them. There was a period when I went out with two at the same time. This is not good, but it had happened with me as a civilian, too, and it's acceptable for me, because in the depth of her heart every woman is a slut, as a well-

known person once said. For more than two weeks I haven't seen any of the guys I know, and that makes me bored.

I received a letter from Misha Rumyantsev – good guy, Deputy Battalion Commander for line training in the 184th Rifle Division, Sen[ior] Lieut[enant].

Oh Christ, Fritzes started making mischief here. They dragged the battalion commander with his deputy [from] the 277th Rifle Division – nice prisoners to be interrogated. The regiment commander has been sent to a penal battalion. If a sniper is taken prisoner, it's a great piece of luck for the enemy, for we know all the armies, let alone the divisions, and we can find anything anywhere. And yet Nesterova and Tanaylova didn't say anything when they were tortured by the Fritzes – good for the girls, even though some called them 'rats'. I saw their pictures in a German newspaper, but those were old photos, from their Red Army service record books. That's enough, I'm going to sleep.

Oh, and I often think about my favorite Arkhangelsk with its foreign sailors, Importclub, Dynamo Stadium, big theater, "Edison," "Ars" and "Victory" cinemas – I can see all its culture and entertainment centers in my mind's eye.

T. V. Kurochkina, Rosa's employer at the kindergarten:

Of course Roza missed all these things. She was a soldier but she was also very young and loved to have fun. She was a good comrade, she liked singing and dancing, and she loved coming up with something funny. I remember her devoting her free time to sports and working in the hospital. She would ask her k[inder]garten colleagues and the children's parents to donate books and tabletop games; she would take newspapers and books to the hospital; she would prepare small performances done by kids.

Roza Shanina:

Zina And[rianova] *is from Alma-Ata, Tosya Kot*[yolkina] *is from Kuybyshev* [now Samara]*, Anya K*[uznetsova] *is from Tatarstan, Tamara Alkh*[imova] *and Kalya are from Moscow: from Taganka and Kropotkinskaya streets. The rest are from Sverdlovsk, Moltovsk (Urals), Arkhangelsk, Siberia (Omsk) – Masha Rozhkova. Finished.*

9 DECEMBER 1944

Everything is alright. In the evening I went to listen to records at the major's, chief of the oper[ations] division. The records were rather sad: "Hour by Hour," "Coachman," and others, and I became overwhelmed with sadness. At first I tried to control myself, but then I just couldn't hold back any longer, and on top of that he teased me, so I howled. I cried so much, and played that record, "Hour By Hour", ten times over. Then he said: "You want some vodka?" I said: "OK! But let me drink a lot, I wanna get drunk." I gathered and prepared a few things: my hat and mirror, and his lantern, so we wouldn't have to search for them later. He poured it in a teacup, very big. I drank it and asked for more, and again, and then I remember absolutely nothing. I didn't even eat anything while I was drinking. "Again," I said. "Hour by Hour" played. Later, I remember, a man came in, an officer, on some official business, so they began to talk. And I took advantage of the opportunity; grabbed my stuff and the lantern and ran out and away, then cried violently all evening, piss drunk. I got up in the morning, very early, feeling bored and having a pounding headache so I ironed all the linen, put everything in order, and again felt sad. I wrote a letter to Comrade Stalin again.

Guys from neighboring positions write me delicate letters, declaring and confessing things, asking me to visit them, but I decided not to go anywhere. I write to them all: "I can't," and delicately explain that I'm not the one and that's all. Nobody cares much about them, but when I leave, people will be talking about me: "Platoon assistant commander," "heroine," etc, so it's better not to get involved. So I sit here alone, feeling sad, and I haven't seen the guys for quite a long time, too, although we live close to each other – 3 km. I write short letters home, with photos and postcards, but I do this very often.

Oh, and today I overheard a conversation between Dusya Krasn[oborova] and Masha Piskunova. They said in front of everyone that we have only three girls [virgins]. I didn't expect this. Oh, Lord, how can I vouch for them? And when did they find the time? [...] They sank to such lows. Among us, I [...] – these are definitely girls, and it is doubtful there are any more. Oh, Lord, so base, so bad, but there's nothing to be done – such are the facts. Not without reason unpleasant things are said about the front women; it's considered weird if one is a girl, in the fullest sense, and that's true.

13 DECEMBER 1944

Yesterday there was a meeting of all the women of the division and an evening party. Many talked about me, saying I showed a good example. Our snipers gave a pretty good concert, Zoya Mikhaylova, Junior Sergeant, *was the entertainer, she is intelligent and cheerful [...]. There was a medical examination of the female snipers, 7 from the platoon turned out to be girls, but how accurate this is, I don't know. [...].*

On the 12th I was wounded. It's amazing; I had a dream in which I was told I'd be wounded. Then I was sitting on the lookout point, and I remembered the dream, and it seemed to me like I was really hurt in the right shoulder. Less than 5 minutes later a Fritz sniper hit me right in the spot where I had seen the wound. I didn't feel much pain, like something was enveloping my whole shoulder. Once bandaged, I didn't require any assistance, so I left for home alone; I didn't want to go to the field hospital, but I was forced to. The surgery was painful. When they finished up, I wanted to go home, back to my unit, but they wouldn't let me go, because I was all stitched up. One would think the wound is no big deal, just two small holes, but they cut it open, so it'll probably take more than a month to heal up.

Now I'm in the hospital; the whole shoulder joint is sore, but not too bad. I'm thinking of running away, but what I will do next, I don't know. I like one of the nurses — well, and a female physician (a major), and the rest here are pretty ignorant. I was invited by the boy snipers to join them for the evening, but alas, I'm not home now, so they will come for me.

18 DECEMBER 1944

Every day I have dreams about my friends Sasha and Kalya. How I miss them! I receive many letters which the girls bring to me (from Karshinov, Borovik, Rumyantsev). All write about their love for me. Vanyushenka is the only one to whom I write good letters from the heart. Nice guy, Senior Sergeant. [...]. I get letters from the girls I studied with; they congratulate me on my success.

I've just came back after watching a film named "Lermontov." What a great effect it had on me! The character of Lermontov is very close to me. I decided to follow his example and do as I like rather than as someone else wants me to do. His silhouette on the iron bridge, the image of a horseman, will remain with me; I want to be first somewhere, too. No one can convince me now, and if I plunge into a difficulty I'll be able to solve the problem any minute, too; for I don't cling to life, I just exist. So let me go rogue, so that not just some but many know what's what. Oh, how I like Lermontov's character!

19 DECEMBER 1944

I'm in the army recovery center. Yes, I want to do something, not to distinguish myself, [but] to satisfy my inner urge or something that torments me. My mood is still the same. I got here in a Willys jeep – there was a major in it, so they gave me a lift. The driver, it turned out, lived near me in Arkhangelsk. He promised to give me a sniper badge, which he'd been given by mistake. He's a tanker.

Here is my portrait[1] from the "Frontline Humor" magazine dated November 7, 1944. Oh, God, I'm so bored. Settled in OK, though. Now I'm going to read the book "Sister Carrie."

———————————————

1. There was a portrait (a magazine image) pasted in the diary. Now there is only a note written in blue ink: "The portrait that was here has been sent to the editors together with the manuscript."

27 DECEMBER 1944

When my life is good, I don't want to write.

While I was in the recovery center, I read "Sister Carrie" and "Bagration." Good books. "Oh Carrie, Carrie! Oh blind strivings of the human heart! Onward, onward, it saith, and where beauty leads, there it follows." When you read this, you think Theodore Dreiser wrote this for you. Or Bagration: "What is glory? It is either getting your own skull split in the name of the Motherland, or crushing the skull of someone else – that's what glory is!" I will do so, by God.

I watched a lot of films: "In Old Chicago," "Wait for Me," etc. "Submarine No. 9." made a better impression on me; I even thought about it a bit. The rest are so-so, I can't say they were good.

. . .

Now I'm at Nikolay Fyodorov's. Just dropped in for no special reason, and probably for the last time, as I do not feel drawn towards him. Why, it's been a month since I last visited him, and haven't even talked to anybody since then. The document for the Order of Glory 1st Cl[ass] has been issued.

Yesterday, a good sweet boy stuck to me like glue: "Let me kiss you. I haven't kissed a girl for 4 years." And he asked so earnestly, I got sentimental. And really, he was so cute, so I didn't feel nasty, but nice. "To hell with you, go ahead and kiss me, but just one time." And I nearly wept. Why? Out of compassion.

8 JANUARY 1945

There was no paper, and I didn't write anything for a long time. After I got out of the recovery center, I went to General Ponomaryov, a mem[ber] of the Milit[ary] Coun[cil], to reach my goal – getting back to the front line. I was sent to the commander of the 5th Arm[y], Colon[el[-Gen[eral] Krylov. With great difficulty I persuaded him to let me return to him on February 5, and he would give me a document allowing me to go on the offensive. I also managed to succeed in getting new uniforms for the girls, as they are poorly dressed. Ponomaryov ordered to do all I asked for, but now I see that his orders are not really carried out properly, and it's all just words. I sat the whole day waiting for Ponomarev to receive me, but I achieved my purpose. I was dressed lightly, so I was given a major's fur coat and taken in a Willys jeep to the medical battalion, which I was happy with. I only managed to get fur coats, valenki boots and camouflage overalls; I froze on the trip, but at least I made it, for it's really cold in the trenches. My overcoat became short, for I've grown bigger this year, and I didn't like it anyway, so I traded it for a telogreika.

I am in the 157th [R.D.] with the girls. I can't recognize them! My friends Sashka and Toska have gotten married. Lord, there are only four girls, no, five remaining out of the twenty-seven. I don't think of doing that, but I'm afraid [of] getting into trouble because some of the girls were raped, so now I don't stay overnight as easily as I did before. But it's hard to sleep in the cold. Today I spent the night at some Lieutenant-Colonel's, and he hit on me asking for a kiss – but I know it always goes further than that. I keep telling lies about myself.

Oh, yes: while I was absent, a good girl, Tanya Kareva, Junior Sergeant, was killed. Her friend Valya L. returned from the hospital after being wounded and found out there was no Tanya anymore, and oh, how Valya cried. Valya Lazarenko: 25, good-natured, lovely, tall, blonde, loves horses very much. She is the best independent girl in the whole platoon. In the past she finished 7 cl[asses], and worked [in] factory-and-workshop education, graduating from a factory apprenticeship school.

. . .

OK, that's all for now; I'm going to fix my watch. When it gets warmer, in February I'll run away to the front line. For repelling a counterattack (it was hot, I risked my life), I was awarded the medal "For Courage."

13 JANUARY 1945

I didn't sleep all night, I feel bad, sick. Germans hit hard. Today our barrage lasted from 9 to 11:05. The Katyushas gave a signal first. We did make it hot for the Fritzes. Now the situation is still unclear. We have itchy feet. Oh, L[ord], how noisy it is in the dug[out!] The dugout is low, it leaks and is filled with smoke; we had to make the bunk beds into single beds. Hardly had we finished the work than we had to advance further. The day is pretty chilly, but it's too wet for felt boots and too cold for kirza boots. Everyone takes short fur coats, but I'm a northerner and don't need one; it is hard to walk wearing it.

14 JANUARY 1945

We started passing through Lithuania and Belorussia. No, our troops will hardly be able to move far; our right flank took Pilikalen yesterday, and today our forces have been pressed again. Our left [flank] has already moved far ahead. But we still hear gunfire. We spent the entire morning listening to the thundering cannonade. The Katyushas heralded the beginning of the grand events. Everyone has gone forward.

There is just one horse wagon left for our platoon, and what are we supposed to do, sleep out in the snow with nothing to warm ourselves with? We can't carry all our things, so we believe it's a matter of principle. Didn't they really have another spare horse for us? Oh, how unnecessary we are, nobody cares about us. We had no

din[ner] *and no breakfast. It's* 12 *o'clock, and we're still
sitting.*

I am considering everyone's behavior. [...]. *Lyuba
Reshetnikova, private* 1st class, *is not in the platoon. She
wen*[t] *ahead with her fellow. Yesterday I wrote to Vovka
Eme*[lya]*nov. Congratulated him on his marriage to my
dear friend Sasha Yekimova. And I wrote that our trio
(Sasha, Kalya, and I) no long*[er] *exi*[s]*ts. I'm out* [of] *it,
as our interests diverged and we have nothing to talk
about. And Sasha read it, too. If I wished to live in the
platoon, then I would become friends with Valya
Lazarenko, but I'm leaving soon to join the company. I
made a pact* [with] *Valya not to talk in army language,
and to not use even a single unprintable word. Whoever
breaks the pact has to give the other her sugar for two
weeks. The girls can cuss you out, and you can't do
anything about it. My dear Sashka has become
undisciplined.*

Marat Shanin, Roza's youngest brother:

Shortly after Sasha married Vovka, his unit was
reassigned to a different part of the front and the
newlyweds were separated. Vovka was given leave to
visit his young wife for International Women's Day on
8 March. Poor Vovka arrived only to discover that
Sasha had been killed two weeks earlier, on 26
February 1945.

On the day of her death, Sasha and her fellow sniper Dusya Kekesheva—who was pregnant—were ambushed by a group of Germans who cut their throats. Sasha was found a short distance from their trench. She had, perhaps, crawled for help or had tried to escape.

The two snipers' bodies were brought to their dugout by their comrades, who held a funeral for them the following day. They were buried in coffins with full military honors.

After learning of his wife's death, Vovka returned to his unit. A month later, he was wounded and died of his wounds on 5 April 1945.

Kalya Petrova[1] survived the war and in 1945 returned to Moscow, where she received a degree in hydrology. She spent the rest of her life working as an academic. Kalya shared many of her front memories and was often interviewed by newspapers and authors.

Roza Shanina:

I wrote a letter home, something like this: "Dear Mother, [...] I had a hard life, and without a minute of hesi[ta]tion left [you] easily in 1938. I hold no grudge, and I don't blame [...], I only beg that if I die, then give Yuliya an education. Please love Yuliya, bec[ause] childhood years are more vividly remembered, and children are a joy."

. . .

I wrote to Nikola[y] Solomatin: "Wherever you [are],
noble falcon, my love is with [you]." I wrote that I don't
have a boyfriend because [of] him, and if I met him now,
he would deceive me. I've become more determine[d]; he
told me so fervently back then that he loved me, and now
he's forgotten me, and I even learned that he has a wife. I
condemned his flattery and hypocrisy, but I wasn't
offended that he didn't love me.

In Valya Lazarenko's album there is a photo of the
city of Chelyabinsk. She's a pretty, young blonde. Her
father, like mine, almost kicked her out of the house. We
are very similar, only I'm less interesting than her, but
she is less educated than me. She envies me [for] that.
"Love stands strong, it gives beauty where there [is]
none, and forges chai[ns] which no spell can bre[ak]."
("The Heart of a Princess"). On the second page she's
like a boy, with cropp[ed] hair, wearing pants and a
soldier's blouse, with a dog, – that's her on the front, the
159th R.D., [19]43. She's terribly fond of horses, and she
wrote: "Being in the cavalr[y] means you must not only
love the business, but you need to have the soul of a
cavalryman." (Ivan Nikulin). After the war, she wants
to stay for life in the cavalry.

Further on, we six standing in Lithuanian costumes, I
and them. They also were a trio. Tanya was killed,
Lyuda wounded, and now she's alone. Here they are in
Valya's album: Lyuda and Tanya with Lyuda's father.
Here is a postcard – a beautiful girl with a horse - which

I gave her before I was wounded. Valya was wounded, too, and we left the hospital together. That's what I wrote: "In memory of the days on the front line, 24.10.4[4]. Remember the march in East Pruss[ia], when we just entered it. What was the base of our lives for us front girls? I came to the conclusion that there is no truth, only lies and hypocrisy. Remember how we were looked at ... Oh, girls, where are we to go, where can we find truth? There is no truth." Back then, when I went forward with the soldiers, I was falsely accused of in[decent] behavior with them. Further on: "Die, but do [not] give a kiss without [love!]" (Chernyshevsky). Here is her poem:

When [I] am whiling away the difficult
    days,
The days when I am separated from my
    family [and] you,
I remember the past longingly,
Discontented with my fate.
Of all my family I stood out
With curiosity and secret thoughts
About races, and raids, and myself on a
    steed,
And my horse was so vigorous and
    playful.
Oh my horse, my dear raven-black
    horse
With a golden silk mane!

In my difficult days,
You were my one true joy.
What a pleasure it is to ride in the
    silence of the night,
Sitting on your back, my eternal
    comrade,
Zipping through the storms and fires
    together,
With fragments of bombs and shells
    whizzing around us.
If you only knew, my friend, how
    faithful I am to you.
You are the only one I fell in love with.
If you knew and if you could speak,
I would talk only to you alone.
Now, lying in a hospital bed,
I cannot forget you.
[A]lone, in secret, I am yearning
For you forever, my love.
Do not be jealous, my hand[some],
You are the only one I love so much.
Though I have to confess that
    some[times]
I fee[l] a little sad over Genka.
I miss him, but he doesn't love me.
I'll share this grief with you.
He probably loves someone else,
Telling her: "You're the only one I
    love."

He told me, too, that he would never
    forget me.
But that could not be for long:
As soon as he disappeared from [view],
He was about to forget me forever.
I don't care, I'll forget everything
About Genka, about my first l[ove].
And I will return to you, my com[rade],
And I will caress you a[gain].

EH 3049, Kaunas[2]. *11.12.*[44.]

It's frosty outside. The cannonade doesn't stop, getting closer and closer, pus[h]*ing on the right* [flank]. *We were ordered to move over to Eydtkuhnen. We chowed down* [a] *bit on some sausages and bread that had been broug*[ht] *to us. Our* [ar]*tillery barrage has been started.*

---

1. Kaleria Pertova died in 2014.
2. Evacuation Hospital 3049 (EH 3049). It was located in Kaunas, Lithuanian SSR, from 01.09.1944 to 08.07.1945.

15 JANUARY 1945

After that we moved [to] *the town of Etkunen, in the rear of the division. This morning everyone was going to the bath, and I put on a* [wh]*ite camouflage cloak, kissed everyone, and now I'm already in the rear near the headquarters of the 144th R.D.; in an hour I'll be on the front line, I've covered 20 km since* [m]*orning. I wrote a nice letter to* [N]*ikolay Borovik – why quarrel, perhaps I will be killed?*

16 JANUARY 1945

I spent the first night at the General's, Donets, Commander of the 144th Rifle Division. *I was received perfectly by him and all the workers. The next day, by noon, I left to look for the regiment. I met Kasimov, but didn't tell him anything, and he didn't recognize me.*

I met the SP gunners; we went on the attack in the tanks. I wa[s] in a tank. One was hit, there were badly wounded men. Major Gubanov was killed, an old acquaintance of Sasha Ye[kimova], 8 times awarded. Everybody felt sorry for him.

In the evening I went to Borovik and got frozen solid. I reached Borovik['s] dugout, not so happy to meet him as to be in a warm dugout. It's frosty in the tank, I'm not accustomed to tank smoke and it hurts my eyes; I can't breathe these fumes. I slept like a log.

Again, the General doesn't allow me to stay on the front line. I went to the 216th R.R., reported; they received me but were suspicious, hardly believing I could've been allowed to go to the front line. Regiment Com[mander] wouldn't let me go there.

I'm finally sure that I'm not capable of love. What a thrill I felt in my heart when I first saw Nik[olay] Borovik. But today I found some flaws in him. Oddly enough, even in wartime my heart does not give concessions. Nikolay had no strap [on] the back of his overcoat, one of his shoulder straps was almost torn off, and so on. I found him a slob, and the feeling of disgust drowned out love. He makes me sick already. He went into battle, and now he's seriously wounded. I feel sorry for him as a warrior, but that's about it.

Everyone in the platoon already knows I was injured, and nobody is looking for me there. But I joined the regiment without Donets' permission, how will I explain that?

. . .

There is an unbearable wind outside, a blizzard, with not just snow [but] even dirt being blown up in the air. The earth is grey, and my camouflage already reveals me, because it's too white, even though dirty. Today I ate nothing all day, and the tank smoke gives me a headache. I'm not assigned for rations anywhere, because I don't have papers, and I'm not registered anywhere yet. The last few days I was half starved; today I'm starving. I do not let myself get sassy, I can somehow do without food for a while; it won't last too long.

I'm taken as a notable sniper; it seems that's the only reason that I've been accepted. But everyone thinks I came because I have a man in this division. The regimental com[mander] even asked this question. I decided not to love anyone, 'cause I don't want to get disappointed again. I came, but I don't know a single soul here. I have to endure dirt, cold, hunger. Those who know me (the tankers, the general) all advise that I should return to the platoon, instead of suffering such a war where I can be killed any moment due to the enemy's dense fire.

I'm very often under fire. On the front line I was also with the infantry in the 785th R.R. commanded by Kasimov. While I was there, all the girls were given white fur coats and valen[k]i boots: so beautiful and warm.

. . .

A few drivers were attached to [our] platoon in the rear of the 157th R.D. for protection. The girls ride in the cabs, see their sweethearts; it's warm, easy and satisfying. This I also want. But some unknown force is pulling me to the front line. Oh, passion, passion! Oh, blind strivings of the human heart! Onward, onward, it saith, and where beauty leads, there it follows. I obey my heart. I like adventures, explosions, and it is particularly interesting to repel counterattacks. Whatever happens, I'll charge onward – it's my last irrevocable charge! But I'm hungry, I've lost weight over the last 3 days, I can feel it.

Now it's evening, so many casualties. It's the same again: in 5 days, we have only moved forward 10 km. The 1st Belorus[sian Front]: in 3 days, 60 km forward and 120 [km] along the fr[ont] line.

I sat and thought for a while, and I'll write some more. Oh, you would bind my will with your laws? The law makes a crawling snail of those who would take off in an eagle's flight.

I have an aura of celebrity. Recently, the army newspaper "Unich[tozhim] Vraga" ["We'll Defeat the

Enemy"] *wrote: "Shanina, who distinguished herself during the enemy's counterattack, has been awarded the medal 'For Courage'. She is a renowned sniper in our unit." In the Moscow magazine "Ogoniok" ["Spark"] my portrait is on the front page: destroyed 54 Germans, captured three, awarded two Orders of Glory – that was before. I picture being read by the whole country, all my friends and acquaintances; and who will know what I feel at this moment.*

Recently, poet Ilya Ehrenburg wrote about me in the army newspaper, thanking Captain Starostenko, the battalion commander, who was the first to enter German territory, as well as Yurgin and me as a notable sniper. "I thank her fifty-seven times over. She has saved the lives of thousands of Soviet people." And I thought to myself, Is this really glory? "Glory is either getting your own skull split in the name of the Motherland, or crushing the skull of someone else – that's what glory is!" (Bagration said), while this is just hogwash for the rear. What have I actually done? No more than I'd have to as a Soviet man, standing up to defend the Motherland.

Today I am willing to go on an attack, even a melee. I have no fear; my own life is repug[n]ant to me. I am glad to die fo[r] the Motherland, it's great that I have this opportunity, or else I'd have had to die a nasty death. So many soldiers are killed!

17 JANUARY 1945

I got up, but had no chance to have breakfast: the top brass came. I went to the battalion. I participated in the attack together with the infantry, in the first ranks. We moved forward but didn't report to the rear, so our Katyusha hit us, together with a fiddler[1] – oh, there was such a bloody mess! It was the first time I experienced so much art[illery] fire. I experienced a lot of machine gun fire for the first time on July 19 with Solomatin on the Neman. And now? This day for me seemed like a month. People all around were hit and torn to pieces; I nearly vomited at all the body parts. I bandaged the wounded and moved forward. I and two others rushed into a white house on the right side, thus completing the objective - but the route of our division changed; we turned left, so the work proved useless.

. . .

The 371st R.D. easily followed us. But there was no further way forward. The Fritzes shot at us with all kinds of weapons. 100 m[eters] away, in a gully behind the house, was the enemy's self-propelled artillery, firing from machine guns and sending shells. A Fritz looked up out of a hatch, and I shot him from the house; but there were no more good targets for the rest of the day.

Frost, hunger. I came to my unit. Some guys throw dirty compliments at me. Filthy language everywhere. I'm so tired. I started looking for my comrades. I came across some acquaintances, then went on to look for the regiment. I stumbled onto the division command post and settled there for the night. It's cold, I have eaten little. I had taken a trophy from the house – this album with paper, in which I want to rewrite everything. My heart is heavy. I see I'm not too useful as a sniper; perhaps there will be opportune moments yet, but there is also a risk of death. There are only 6 left out of 78 in our 2nd B[attalio]n of the 216th R.R. I miss the girls, and my life now is much worse than theirs.

I've been sitting and crying for the last three hours. It's midnight. Who needs me? What good am I? I can't be of any help. Nobody wants to know how upset I get about things. It seems like there are too many of those who sympathize with me, but none of them really offers any help. I don't know what to do next. I often hear dirty talk. For what do I deserve such useless torture? All I hear is shouting raunchy things and cussing, I don't talk to anyone. Suddenly I was asked, "Is your name Shanina?" I didn't answer. It turned out it was the best friend of Pavel Blokhin; I knew him well, but now I didn't recognize him. What a pleasant meeting. He's Ch[ief] of Reconnaissance for the 785th R.R. He said, "I've been told Shanina was awarded orders." I said my name was Klava, and I heard many unpleasant comments. I really liked j[unior] l[ieutenan]t Nikolay, he was very considerate to me.

---

1. "Fiddler" (military slang), a German six-barrelled rocket launcher.

24 JANUARY 1945

I haven't written anything for a long while. There was no time. I went to the reconnaissance platoon in Regiment 785. Wonderful guys; they welcomed me nicely, but the chief of the regiment headquarters started to harass me, being mean to me for nothing, grabbing at me as if I were a brothel whore. I couldn't stand it and swore at him. After that, I only stayed there for two days and then left: it was impossible to live there anymore because the harassment intensified.

During those two days, there was no time to catch my breath. There was dreadful fighting. The Germans had filled their trenches with infantry and armed them, and they fought us off resolutely. Our troops went past the trenches and stopped at an estate 150-200 meters away. The Fritzes fired whenever they passed by. It was complete carnage. So many times our infantrymen were put on self-propelled artillery to be taken to that estate, but each time only 1 or 2 could reach it, and the rest were mowed down [by enemy fire]. I took a ride in one self-propelled gun but didn't even have a chance to shoot: you couldn't stick your head out of the hatch without being killed or wounded. I managed to get closer through the gully, crawled out and fired at Fritzes fleeing from the trench.

By the evening of the 22nd we had kicked them all out and occupied the estate. We went forward, but there was an antitank ditch. I went on. The infantry were lying on the ground, afraid to advance. Two shtrafbat scouts were going ahead, and I went with them. As a result, the three of us were the first to take the next estate, and the rest of the soldiers came in on the attack behind us and started nipping at the heels of the fleeing Fritzes. I was firing, like everyone else. But it turned out that those shtrafbat soldiers were our left-flank neighbors, the 63rd R.D.

The commanders of the 63rd R.D., as they saw me, shouted to the soldiers, "Follow the example of this girl, learn to be like her." They wanted to make me stay with them, but I went to look for my comrades-in-arms. As I ran, I screamed to some soldiers on the right, "Which division?" And I heard them shout from behind, "Halt!" And to the left, 4 meters from me, two Fritzes stood up out of the bush[e]s with their hands up.

. . .

I met the divisional scouts and they sheltered me, saying, "You will come with us." And we led the others forward, to the west. We captured 14 stray Fritzes and marched on. The Fritzes retreated without looking back, and then we were suddenly ordered to return and turn right. We rode in trucks, and there were our columns marching, all heading to the town of Schlusselburg. We passed the town and went on further. Here the Germans had ditched everything (cows and all) and fled into the woods. They keep firing at the village. Sometimes German Fraus are met. Our guys give them rides on tractors, etc. [...]. And, oh God, how many vehicles do we have! The whole army is on the move, and there are many complaints that hardly anyone follows traffic rules.

A big iron bridg[e] over a river. A beautiful road, good overlook on the meadows. There are a bunch of downed trees near the bridge; the Germans wanted to make an abatis[1] but didn't have enough time. Luxurious stone houses, elegant furnishings everywhere: pianos, big mirrors, silk, plush or lace curtains, beautiful chairs and all the furniture. The scouts have no time to keep me company, they're busy with their work, and there is no place to sleep anyway, so they leave me.

I was in the division. There was Vadim, a lieutenant, son of Headquarters Chief Colonel. This Mamma's little darling just hangs about doing nothing, but he is really mean. He stuck close to me: "Let me kiss you," he was drunk, so he took it into his head. I was in the middle of changing my camouflage pants. He just walked in without permission and wouldn't let me put on my pants. Small but strong. He twisted my arms around, threw me down on the couch, kissing me, and just then the Colonel walked in – his father. I was in tears, crying. "What's going on?" I say, "Just because I'm a girl, does that mean everyone has to kiss me?" He yelled at his son, but after he had left, Vadim said, "Understand, I don't want German women, they're infected, and you're a clean, pretty girl, and I still want to kiss you." I said, "There are many who want the same, and what am I supposed to become because of you all?"

Another night-time march. It is dark now; soon it will be dawn. I am sitting by the campfire, writing. How bad it feels when I have no superior officer. It is good not to be ordered about, but not good when there is no one to advise me what to do. My heart finds no contentment. Nobody needs me.

[The end of Roza's diary].

---

1. A field fortification consisting of an obstacle formed of the branches of trees laid in a row, with the sharpened tops directed outwards, towards the enemy.

EPILOGUE

Marat Shanin, Roza's youngest brother:

How sad, reading the last words committed in her diary. *Nobody needs me.* How wrong she was...my dear sister. Her Motherland needed her, her family needed her, and apparently, God too, needed her by His side. Yet how sad that she quit this world thinking that...

On January 27th, 1945, only three days after her last diary entry, and only three months short of Adolf Hitler's death, my beloved sister was severely wounded by a shell fragment in the stomach, and a day later, on January 28th, she died of her wounds in the hospital of the 205th Medical Battalion.

In her last twenty-four hours of life, her courage and bravery shone brighter than ever. In a letter sent to me, Nikolay Lyantsev, Senior Sergeant and Commander, Full Cavalier of the Order of Glory, wrote of how he had discovered my wounded sister. He and a telephone operator heard a heartrending woman's scream and ran to help whoever it was. As they reached the wounded woman, they saw it was Roza. He wrote:

"She was lying on the ground, awake. As soon as she saw us she begged: 'Guys, dear, please shoot me, quick!' Her stomach was torn open, and she tried to hold her insides in with both hands."

The two soldiers bandaged her and carried her off the battlefield.

Yekaterina Radkova, the nurse at the hospital where Roza was taken, described to me my sister's last moments.

"Even in her terrible condition she remained herself – no groaning, no tears. She was very thirsty, but she wasn't allowed to drink anything. She would ask me: 'Katya, give me some lovely cold water. I'll just rinse my mouth ...' And when I gave her water, she did only rinse her mouth. The other wounded soldiers that had fought together with her (I guess it was 612nd Rifle Regiment) told me how she had been wounded. There had been very heavy fighting. The enemy penetrated the area where Roza was, the commander was killed, and then she rose to her feet and led the soldiers into the battle. The penetration was eliminated, but Roza was badly wounded. Despite her serious state, she had a soothing influence on the wounded men and was an example of courage and dignity. Roza understood how grave her condition was. She wanted to live too! When she felt very bad, she asked me to sit beside her, and she spoke about her home and her friends. 'I don't want to die,' Roza said. 'I've seen so little and done so little ...'"

The hospital staff sent Roza's death notification to the school where she had worked. It was received by Roza's former employer T.V. Kurochkina.

T.V. Kurochkina, Roza's former employer:

The notification of her death sent by the hospital staff was addressed directly to me. They explained in their letter why they wrote me: Roza had often mentioned my name during her illness, and there was only my address found in her belongings. The address on the notification was from the girls' dormitory where Roza had lived as a student, not her mother's. I cried as I read that incredible paper announcing the death of that young girl, still in the prime of life when taken so viciously from us. It read:

> 205th Medical-Sanitary Battalion
> 11 February, 1945
> rec'd 1 March, 1945
> Notification
> Please notify Shanina, Anna Alexsandrova,

resident in city of Arkhangelsk, 15 Leningrad Avenue, that her daughter Sn. Sergeant Shanina, Roza, in battle for the Socialist Motherland, in loyalty to the military oath, showing heroism and honor, was wounded and died from wounds on 28 January, 1945.

Buried with full military honors East Prussia Richau 3km south-east of Ilmsdorf village.

In their letter, the hospital staff members wrote that they made every effort to save Roza's life, but all was in vain. They also wrote that they tried to give her as good a burial as possible. When Roza was carried out of the hospital, Chopin's Funeral March was played on the piano.

Shortly afterwards, I was summoned to the Pervomaysky recruitment office. There I was officially informed of her death and that they had received her belongings. I had to offer them an explanation as to why I had been involved as addressee, and I gave them her parents' address. Just a little earlier, after much thought, I had written a letter to her mother. I had selected some of Roza's letters, as well as the death notification received from the hospital, with the description of her funeral and the information on the place where she was buried. I sent all those to her mother together with my own letter.

Soon I got a reply from Roza's mother. I guess you can imagine what a mother who sent five children to the war can write. It was difficult to understand from her letter whether she had lost all of them.

Shortly before the end of the war, I received another letter from a lad still serving in the army. He asked me about Roza and wrote that he and Roza dreamed of being together after the war. I had to reply to him and let him know the sad news. He sent me another letter in which he expressed his grief and wrote many good things about Roza. But it was so long ago that I forgot both his first and last name, and I lost his letters during moving from one place to another.

Marat Shanin:

I was barely seventeen years old when my brave sister died. And soon after her, our brother Sergey was killed. They died within a week of each other.

It wasn't until 1965, however, that we learned about the circumstances of his death. It took more than twenty years for the government to send Sergey's death notification to my family. Upon his arrest and after his confession, the Special Council of the USSR NKGB sentenced Sergey to be shot with confiscation of property. The sentence was carried out on February 3rd, 1945. He was killed by a Soviet bullet. Rather than fight the Nazis, Sergey was fighting against his own people, who ultimately killed him. He was only 33 years old, and left two small daughters and a grieving wife behind.

We knew he had died, of course, but to learn the truth after a staggering two decades was heart-wrenching. But that's how it was then. The individual had no real power. Even if one believed one had it, and tried to voice it, one soon learned just how wrong one was. I remember an incident related to me by my mother while I was still very young. She said that long before I had been born, she used to attend the meetings of the communist party in our village. At one such meeting my poor mother had asked, "How on earth can poor villagers pay such taxes?" No sooner did she utter the question than a murmur of disproval filled the gathering. To escape imprisonment, my father ran to her aid. He told her to butcher her cow, load the meat on a sledge and deliver it to Shangaly. My poor frightened mother did as she was told. She killed her cow and used the meat to bribe the authorities. It was the last time she ever visited political gatherings.

After we received the death notification of my sister Roza, my mother decided to take me and my young sister Yuliya—the only children who remained with her —and follow our father to Solista, where he had moved to take up his role as Party Organizer of the Arkhangelsk Regional Committee of the Communist Party. It was a brave move on my mother's part, to leave everything behind—including her sad memories. Or that's what I thought. But it wasn't to be. I believe that no matter how far she would have gone, my mother never was quite able to leave the memories of her dear children lost to our country behind. They stayed with her, as they would with any other mother.

And Roza was always in her thoughts. I remember she once said, *"Maybe it's for the best that she's died. Otherwise, how would she have been able to live after the war? She shot so many people."*

I felt my blood run cold when I heard Mother's words about Roza. After all these years, I can still hear them. She felt with a mother's heart the utter hopelessness of her heroic daughter's fate.

One year later, in 1946, we moved yet again, this time to Krasnoyarsk, where my brother Pavel lived. Life was hard there after the war. Bread tickets, no kitchen garden of our own. Mother would ask me, "Maratko, what kind of government is this anyway? They wouldn't even offer me a mere ruble as a pension!"

Mother died in November 1964. She was 73 years old. I stayed with her in her last moments. She waved her arms saying, "He's far away ..." Then she fell silent, thinking about something, looking dead serious. I didn't dare to interrupt. Then she suddenly said, "Why, Marat is a handsome lad!" So she did recognize me after all. But I cannot say the same thing about Pavel. To his heart-felt distress, Mother did not recognize him before she died.

Our strong, cruel, demanding father, Yegor the Lame, followed Mother only four years later. He went to his grave criticizing Khrushchev, the premier, holding him responsible for the de-Stalinization of the Soviet Union.

.   .   .

Fedya's body was never recovered. Roza and Sergey
went to their deaths without knowing what had become
of our brother. Not even twenty years later, as it was in
Sergey's case, did we learn the circumstances of Fedya's
death. *We're going to have a big battle tomorrow,* he
wrote in his last letter to me. I am certain that he had
lost his life in that big battle. It was decided to consider
him missing as from December 1942.

I still hold his letters sent from the front in a special
drawer. And no matter how many years pass, I now and
then pull them out and reread them. The courage with
which he threw himself into battle always brings tears
to my eyes. But it is the enthusiasm in his letters that
softens my sadness, for no matter how unfair and tragic
his fate had been, I know at least that he was happy to
be a soldier, to fight for our country. Here is one such
letter, a written statement of my brother's bravery.

"Greetings, my dear parents, Father Yegor
Mikhailovich, Mother Anna Alexeyevna, brothers
Misha and Marat, sisters Roza and Yuliya!

First of all, I want to let you know that, from the
very first day when Hitler the Bandit treacherously
invaded the Soviet land, I have been on the front
lines. I am fulfilling my solemn duty to my
Motherland. We pound the enemy with accurate
artillery fire. That puts me in good spirits. My heart
is full of resentment for the vile Nazis who

disrupted the peaceful working life of millions of Soviet people.

I swear to you, and I swear to the Communist Party and the Soviet Government, that I will continue to beat the Nazi bastards with precise artillery fire. I will spare neither my strength nor my blood, and if needs be, I will give my life to win a complete victory over the enemy. The foul Nazis will be destroyed together with their Hitler.

My dear parents, raise your labor productivity even more. Reap a good harvest with no losses – this way you'll help us front-line soldiers.

Tell my fellow villagers, especially young people, that they should learn how to shoot straight. Tell them to focus on preparing themselves for joining the Red Army, and to keep working with devotion on the collective farm.

Dear Mother, don't worry about me. I feel great. We're fighting the most righteous war. Our case is just, and we'll be victorious. You can be proud, Mother, that your son is bravely defending the Soviet land on the front lines.

I wish you good health and a happy life. Rest assured that your son will accomplish his mission honorably.

I will come home with victory. I remain alive and well.

Your son Fedya."

Both Fedya's and Misha's names were immortalized on the monument to the soldiers fallen in the Great Patriotic War at the school in Yedma, as well as in the Memorial Book of the Krasnoyarsk Region.

At one point, I too, wanted to run to the front. It was in 1943, and I had just been rejected by the Arkhangelsk Nautical School because of some eye problem. When I mentioned the front to my mother, she looked at me with harrowing grief for her killed children and quietly said: "Maratko! What about Yulka and me?" There was so much sadness in her words that I gave up the idea at once, and instead remained behind, helping Mother as much as I could.

After Stalin died, I took a job as Secretary of the Committee of Young Communist League, which I held for several years. After that, I was, by turns, Manager at the Krasnoyarsk Woodworking Plant, Director of the Klyuchi Woodworking Plant, sales and purchasing manager at the Kamchatka Regional Executive Committee, member of the Union of Journalists of the USSR, then of Russia.

But the most important job, perhaps the one I was born to undertake, was to preserve the memory of my sister and brothers who had not returned from the war. This became my life's work. The most important one.

But no matter how important my job was it was they, the fallen heroes, who brought the most important contribution to the world: their sacrifice that permitted us our independence. They died so we could be free.

And that job was one that no other could have overshadowed.

ROZA'S LETTERS 1944

**Letters sent to Pyotr Molchanov, the War
Corespondent**

July 29th, 1944

"Please take this to the administration and assist me.
You know how passionately I want to be with the
fighters at the front and kill Nazis. And here,
imagine, instead of at the front lines – at the rear.
And recently, we lost another 4 black and 1 red[1]. I
want to avenge them. I ask you to talk to someone in
charge, although I know that you are very busy."

August 8th, 1944

"I recently went AWOL. Carelessly left the rear for a company at the front. They did not look for me. Good people have said that leaving from the rear to go to the front is not a crime. And I know that our training company will not go on the offensive, and will stay behind. I also need to be at the front, to see with my own eyes what it is, a real war. And then, to look for the lead battalion? All around the forests and swamps, Germans staggered. It was a dangerous walk. I went to the battalion, which was directed to the front, and on the same day fought in the battle. Beside me, people were dying. I fired, and successfully. And afterwards captured 3 ... these fascists are strong.

I'm happy I went AWOL. Although they reprimanded me. I even got a punishment from the Komsomol – put on watch."

August 31, 1944

"Thank God, finally we are back in the fight. All went to the front. Score increases. I have the most – 42 dead little Hitlers, Ekimova – 28, Nikolaeva – 24."

November 1st, 1944

"Day before yesterday buried girlfriend-in-arms Sasha Koreneva. Two more of our girlfriends were wounded: Lazarenko Valya and Shmeleva Zina. Maybe you remember them?"

November 3rd, 1944

"Returned from the front completely exhausted. This war will be remembered. 4 times the town passed from hand to hand. 3 times I got out from under the noses of the fascists. In truth, war on enemy territory is a serious matter."

November 15th, 1944

"Do not go on the 'hunt' now. Sitting without boots. Movement at the front. Our girlfriends were awarded. Yesterday we gave Sasha an Honorary Diploma of the Central Committee of Komsomol."

November 26th, 1944

"Now in the reserve regiment. We are resting again. Soon forget what it's like to advance. I understand the thirst of my life – battle. But what again? I cannot get my way. Sent here, where I rarely even shoot. And now made-up holidays. Sasha and Lida lie in the bunk and sing "Yes, Hour by Hour Day Passes". Their song spoiled my mood even more."

December 17th, 1944

"Goodbye to treatment. The wound is still worrying. I was sent to the army rest home. It's actually good there. But I want to discuss it with them. They did not ask if the hospital might be better? From the hospital I might command a battalion, and not the sniper platoon. Why do I want to leave the platoon? Not because it didn't take. My character is quite good, with many friends, although, obviously, there will always be disputes. But it's still too quiet there. I already want to work again. This is my need, instinct. How do you explain that? Well, you know, I long for battle every day, every minute. I can be more useful for our common cause."

The letter Roza wrote to her friend Masha, but never sent it

"Greetings, Masha!
Sorry for calling you that, but I don't know your

patronym.1 I decided to write when I accidentally learned about your letter to Claudia Ivanovna.

You write that you are crazy in love with Claudia's husband. And she has a 5-year-old kid. You ask her forgiveness for letting such a thing happen, but that you are going to build a life with her husband. You justify yourself by writing that no one else will raise his child, which you are pregnant with, and that you did not know that N.A. had a wife and child.

You write: "What would I tell his child, when he asks "where's Papa?'" But what answer will Claudia give her son, who already knows his father well, when after the war he asks: "Why did Papa not come home?"

Maybe you are seriously now in love with a soldier you met by accident on the road, but how can Claudia Ivanovna forget her beloved husband?

Who am I? Like you I came to the front. I'm a sniper. Recently I was in the rear. On the tracks, in the train, I was thanking the people who came to see my medals. But they told me all sorts of gossip. Why? Why do others look strangely at a girl in a tunic? For that you are to blame, Masha. I could not find a place then, I can't calm down, and now I'm returning to the front.

I often wonder how we military women will come back from the war. How will we be greeted? Possibly with suspicion, despite the fact that we risked our lives and many of us were killed in battles for the Motherland. If that happens, I blame those who couldn't even fight off foreign husbands.

Think, that you will not be forgiven not only by Claudia Ivanovna, but by all of us. And there are many of us. That's everything I wanted to say.

-Roza Shanina"

---

1. 4 killed and 1 wounded

RESOURCES:

- N.V. Ipatova, A.A. Istomin and V.P. Mamonov, Oktyabrsky, *The brave girl from Ustya*, Arkhangelsk Reg., Ustya Museum of Local Lore, 2016
- Vinogradova, Lyuba. *Avenging Angels*, New York: MacLehose Press, 2017
- Rozas letters as well as information about the fate of Roza's fellow snipers Alexandra Ekimova, Kaleria Petrova, and Dusya Kekesheva were retrieved on January 30th, 2020 from: https://rozasdiary.com/category/uncategorized/

ALSO BY A. G. MOGAN

- Daughter of Paris: *The Diary of Marie Duplessis, France's Most Celebrated Courtesan*
- The S-Bahn Murderer: The Hunt for, and Confession of Paul Ogorzow, Nazi Germany's Most Notorious Serial Killer
- The Secret Journals Of Adolf Hitler: *The Anointed* (*Volume 1*)
- The Secret Journals Of Adolf Hitler: *The Struggle* (*Volume 2*)
- Love on Triple W: *A Heartbreaking True Story About Love, Betrayal, and Survival*
- Humorous History: *An Illustrated Collection Of Wit & Irony From The Past*
- Tragic History: *A Collection of Some of the Most Catastrophic Events in Human History*

ABOUT THE AUTHOR

A. G. MOGAN has always loved history and the personalities that were born of bygone eras. Her interest for the world and its people fueled her passion for human analytics. She's used her knowledge to analyze people and their behavior throughout her adult career, including using her in-depth research to craft poignant biographical novels that readers eagerly devour.

When not studying great historical figures or long-lost stories from the past, she can be found at her home in Europe, enjoying the spoils of a wonderfully ordinary family life.

To learn more, please visit the author's website at
www.AGMogan.com

THANK YOU

Thank you for purchasing this book! It means the world to me. If you enjoyed reading it, or otherwise found it entertaining or useful, kindly leave a short review on Amazon. That helps me tremendously.

A. G. Mogan

Made in the USA
Monee, IL
20 December 2021

86606477R00121